C000139626

H
ch

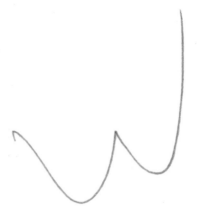

DAVID FREEMANTLE

# How to choose

Why our greatest successes
are a reflection of our small
everyday choices

| BRE | BRI | DIA | GRE | HAG | H/L |
| --- | --- | --- | --- | --- | --- |
| MAR | MOB | | | | |
| 8/02 | | | | | |
| BRA | CH | CHU | EDG | HEC | H/T |
| RED | HLS | | CL | CB | CR |

Prentice
Hall

BUSINESS

*An imprint of* Pearson Education

London • New York • Toronto • Sydney • Tokyo • Singapore • Hong Kong • Cape Town
New Delhi • Madrid • Paris • Amsterdam • Munich • Milan • Stockholm

PEARSON EDUCATION LIMITED

Head Office:
Edinburgh Gate
Harlow CM20 2JE
Tel: +44 (0)1279 623623
Fax: +44 (0)1279 431059

London Office:
128 Long Acre
London WC2E 9AN
Tel: +44 (0)20 7447 2000
Fax: +44 (0)20 7240 5771
Website: www.business-minds.com
          www.yourmomentum.com

First published in Great Britain in 2002

ISBN 0 273 65651 1

British Library Cataloguing in Publication Data
A CIP catalogue record for this book can be obtained from the British Library

10 9 8 7 6 5 4 3 2 1

Designed by Claire Brodmann Book Designs, Lichfield, Staffs
Typeset by Northern Phototypesetting Co. Ltd, Bolton
Printed and bound in Great Britain by Bell & Bain Ltd, Glasgow

The Publishers' policy is to use paper manufactured from sustainable forests.

**Dedication**

To my dear mother Nora who was the original writer in the family. I think she passed her literary genes on to my brother Mike (who is also a writer) and to me.

# About the author

**Dr David Freemantle** gained his doctorate at London University before becoming a production manager with Mars Ltd. He had a meteoric career progression culminating with a position on the board of British Caledonian Airways. In 1985 he founded his own company Superboss Ltd, which specializes in the areas of motivation, leadership and customer relations. He travels the world speaking at conferences and running seminars and has gained an international reputation for his thought-provoking talks and programmes. His clients include major airlines, retail chains, banks and government organizations. This is David's eleventh book. His previous books have been published in 17 different languages and include *The Stimulus Factor* (FT Prentice Hall 2001), *What Customers Like About You* (Nicholas Brealey 1998) and *Eighty Things You Must Do to be a Great Boss* (McGraw-Hill 1995). He lives in Windsor with his wife Mechi, daughter Ruth-Elena and stepdaughter Linnet. He can be contacted at **team@ superboss.co.uk**.

# Contents

# Preface

## Choice

Success in life and
Happiness in general
Is a reflection of the
Choices we make;
Not the big choices
That face us once in a while
But the myriad small choices
That present themselves to us every day


The choices we make are few and far between
Most of the time we do no more than choose
What we have chosen before.
We put ourselves on 'auto-choice'


For every choice we make
There are more than 10,
Sometimes 100, sometimes 1,000
Other options
We are unaware of
But from which we can choose.
Each of these options has to be stimulated
To bring it to a conscious level

By increasing the range of options from which we choose
We increase the probability of choosing success and happiness.
Conversely, by restricting our choices, we limit ourselves

**The big things in our lives and at work**
**Are determined by the small things**
**We choose to do and say**

**HERE ARE SOME OF OUR EVERYDAY CHOICES**

| We can choose our | We can choose to be |
|---|---|
| Assumptions | Critical |
| Bosses | Emotional |
| Expertise | Communicative |
| Relationships | Happy |
| Maxims | Responsive |
| Memories | **Ourselves**        **etc.** |

**This book is aimed at helping you learn**

# How to choose

# Acknowledgments

As always my wife Mechi has provided invaluable support in helping me with my writing. This book will be that much better for her scrutiny. I would also like to thank the team at Pearson for their help, especially Rachael Stock, my editor.

# PART ONE

# Introduction

**Chapter 1** presents an overview of HOW TO CHOOSE.

**The remaining three parts break down as follows:**

**Part 2** consists of six chapters which develop the central thesis of this book, namely that 'our greatest successes are a reflection of our everyday choices'.

**Part 3** consists of three chapters focusing on the HOW TO CHOOSE method.

**Part 4** is a series of 22 short chapters providing a selection of practical applications of this method.

CHAPTER ONE

# Overview: 'How to choose'

> **"**Two roads diverged in a wood, and I –
> I took the one less travelled by,
> And that has made all the difference.**"**
>
> *The Road Not Taken*, Robert Frost (1875–1963)

You are neither just what you eat nor just what you think. The person you are is the total sum of all the choices you have made in life, including choosing to read this paragraph.

## Everything we do is a choice

Everything we do and achieve at work is the result of the choices we make every day. Our performance, our successes, our failures, our relationships with customers and with employees reflect these choices. These choices are often infinitesimally small, often subconscious and often made in defiance of the logical decisions we profess to make. Yet it is these choices that can have a serial impact on the outcomes of our work as well as our lives.

You are here reading this book not just because you made a decision to purchase it in a bookstore or on the web or to borrow it from a library or colleague but as a result of earlier choices you made, choices of how to spend precious moments of your time and choices of where to cast your eye, what to look out for and what to talk about. The topics you choose to take an interest

**It is the choices we make that can have a serial impact on the outcomes of our work as well as our lives.**

in are a reflection of the type of person you choose to be. Not everyone chooses to read this book. In fact, in typical bookstores there are 100,000 other titles to choose from. Why choose this one? Why not that one?

The same applies to our jobs and the very tasks we undertake every minute of the working day. Whatever prescription our employer offers by way of rules, regulations and procedures the choice is ours: whether or not to conform, whether or not to answer the telephone, whether or not to greet a certain person, whether to leave the door open or shut it and even whether or not to have a door. The choice is ours.

## We have unlimited choices every day

While our world is limited physically it is boundless when it comes to the possible choices we have in our everyday lives. By pushing back the boundaries we expose ourselves to more options from which to choose and thus increase the probability of a richer and more fulfilling life. By reining in the choices to a limited routine of repeated activities we restrict our opportunities for fulfilment and put ourselves at risk of predation.

**By pushing back the boundaries we expose ourselves to more options from which to choose and thus increase the probability of a richer and more fulfilling life.**

The choices we make and do not make rarely conform to the logics of scientific decision making. Here am I, in the middle of a 14-hour, night-time flight, being flown by an airline which suffered a major crash with many fatalities less than two weeks ago. It was my choice to fly with this airline. A survey in today's local newspaper indicates that 19% of those questioned would choose not to fly this airline as a result of the crash. Logic plays little part in such choices. If logic were dominant we would all make the same choices in life. But we don't because there are stronger and more powerful forces at play in our lives. These are the emotional and spiritual forces that evolve from the central cores of our 'selves' as human beings and which have a major influence on ALL the choices we make.

# Customer choice

Customer choice is equally fickle as it bears little relation to logic despite the assertions of scientific management. Customer choice reflects myriad individual personal circumstances including the way we allow ourselves to be influenced by a multiplicity of formal and informal choices made by the executives who run a company followed by the frontline people

**On whose behalf do we choose to act?**

who choose to act (and therefore choose their act) on their behalf. On whose behalf do they (and we) choose to act? These are key choices for any business. They are not easy choices.

# Subconscious choice

It might seem contradictory to assert that subconscious choice is automatic. If it is subconscious and automatic how can it be a choice? The answer is that we allow ourselves to be programmed with preset choices. The conscious process of choosing an option is time consuming and often cumbersome, so rather that expend energy unnecessarily by repeating the same conscious choosing process over and over again we programme it into our subconscious so that we automatically choose 'vegetarian' or 'non-smoking' or 'this route' or 'this brand' or 'this company' (without having to think why). These preset subconscious choices are effectively not choices at all.

While subconscious choice is automatic, any conscious choice has to be stimulated. In a previous book, *The Stimulus Factor*, I examined the impact of a range of 17 different stimulus clusters on motivation. In conscious mode choice is the outcome response to any stimulus. We choose how to respond to the stimulus of a rebuke or a word of praise. If we do not think about our response then we respond automatically. These are commonly known as 'knee-jerk' reactions or instinctive behaviours. We act without thinking.

**The more we become conscious of these choices, the more we can influence the outcome of our life and what we do at work.**

Our choices, whether subconscious or conscious, have a tremendous impact on the way we work and on our relationships with others. The more we become conscious of these choices, the more we can influence the outcome of our life and what we do at work.

## The randomness of choice

Soon I will be giving a keynote talk at a major conference in Asia. It's not that I made a decision to pursue this speaking engagement or that the conference organizers made a decision to pursue me. That's too logical. The reason I will be speaking is that I attended another conference a few months ago and heard a young woman speak. I was so impressed I chose to approach her at the end of her session and congratulate her. We got talking and she chose to ask me about my work. Then she chose to mention my name to a colleague who was organizing a forthcoming conference. Had I not chosen to approach this woman I would not be speaking at this forthcoming conference. These random encounters often have a major impact on our lives. Progress can often be made by increasing the amount of randomness we experience in life.

At an in-house workshop I was running for a major retail client recently one of the participants was a supervisor who had volunteered to stand in for her manager who was unable to attend. It was her choice to volunteer (others did not). At the workshop she chose to speak up and make some very constructive suggestions. She made a great impression on everyone present and a month later was promoted to managerial level. She did not choose to seek promotion, all she did was choose to volunteer to deputize for her boss and then choose to speak up at the workshop. She chose to think differently from the rest and in doing so extend the range of options from which to choose (by attending a workshop her colleagues did not she created an increased number of options for herself – options such as speaking up at the workshop, such as getting to know her bosses better).

## Microbehaviours and macrobehaviours

The outcome of our lives are thus the results of a series of such small choices. Many of these choices I call microbehaviours. They are the very small things we do in life – like watching out for a simple opportunity and seizing it (as in the example in the previous paragraph). One thing always leads to another although often we know not what. Thus a microbehaviour (such as speaking up) can lead to an outcome we had not foreseen. We increase the probability of attaining desired outcomes (such as getting promoted) by extending the range of microbehaviours we choose. The greater the range of choices we create

> **The greater the range of choices we create for ourselves the greater the probability the choice we make will lead to success.**

for ourselves the greater the probability the choice we make will lead to success. Conversely, the more we limit ourselves to the same old routines and repetitive behaviours the more restricted our outcomes become.

It is not as if the outcomes we desire in life and at work (such as becoming number one) are always the result of a conscious attempt to implement step by step a plan for achieving this long-term vision (to be number one). It rarely works that way. More often than not the outcome results from a series of short-term short-sighted choices. J.K. Rowling never planned to be number one. She just had an idea about Harry Potter and started writing. One small choice led to another.

## Extending the range of options from which to choose

However, we can increase the probability of achieving desired outcomes by extending the range of options from which to choose. The more bread we sprinkle on water, the greater the probability a fish will bite, but we will never know which fish and when. However, the probability is a fish will bite. If we choose never to sprinkle bread on water a fish will never bite. Similarly, by increasing the number of conscious options from which to choose the greater the probability of a fulfilling outcome.

> **The more bread we sprinkle on water, the greater the probability a fish will bite, but we will never know which fish and when.**

Most times we are in automatic mode and unaware of the choices presented to us. We could choose to go naked to work on a hot summer's day, but who of us do? We are not even aware of this potential choice, therefore we do not consider it. The example is extreme but every minute of every day we are immersed in tens, if not hundreds, if not thousands of options from which to choose and of which we are mostly unaware. Thus we can choose whether or not to greet visitors personally at the entrance as soon as we are notified of their arrival or we can choose to have them sent up to our office. Within these macrobehaviours are 100 potential microbehaviours relating to the hundreds of different ways we can greet people. Thus a macrobehaviour might be choosing to greet a visitor at the entrance while the microbehaviours are the eye movements, gestures and words we choose to put into this greeting. Each of these macro- and microbehaviours will add up to the positive or negative impact we make on our visitors. Our performance will be determined accordingly.

For example, a salesperson has the option of calling a recent customer to enquire how she is getting along with her purchase. While the call itself is a macrobehaviour, how the call is conducted comprises a series of microbehaviours consisting of tone of voice, degree of emotion shown, topics discussed and choice of humour (if any). These all accumulate to yield a desired or undesired outcome with respect to customer satisfaction.

Such macro- and microbehaviours (follow-up calls and what goes into them) are a matter of choice. Few salespeople exercise this choice. Follow-up calls are rare. My own study of successful salespeople reveals that those who sell most are those that follow up most. There is an extended range of macrobehaviour and microbehaviour options available by which salespeople can choose to follow up. These can be by e-mail, telephone, writing, personal visit or invitation to an event. The salesperson has first to choose the macrobehaviour of 'following up' and then has to choose the microbehaviours that comprise the follow-up.

What time to start work in the morning and what time to finish is a personal choice. Who to talk to and who not to talk to is a personal choice. Whether or not to have lunch and with whom is a personal choice. What to say is a personal choice. Virtually everything we do is a reflection of personal choice, yet most of the time we are unaware of these choices. Again, I would stress that these choices will determine our successes and failures in life.

Our life is creaking with so many potential choices, but the paradox is that most times we do not even give them a second's thought. We just do things without thinking. That, of course, is our choice.

The art of everyday choice is to raise to a conscious level the choices we make and to push back the boundaries of possibilities in choosing the appropriate option. We can choose to change our way of working or stay the same, we can choose to improve ourselves or not, we can choose to influence others or remain silent, we can choose our enthusiasms, passions, irritations and grudges. In fact, we can choose most of the things we do in our lives. What we cannot do is choose the actual *outcome*. We can choose a desired outcome and choose to move in that direction, but the outcome is rarely guaranteed. Frequently, the outcome is beyond our control. All we can do is choose the behaviours that move us in the direction of the desired outcome. No soccer team is guaranteed the outcome of a win. All the players can do is choose a strategy and then choose with each kick of the ball how to play the game. As we shall see later randomness is a significant factor in determining the outcome.

**Our life is creaking with so many choices.**

## Choosing partners

Just to be controversial for a moment I would assert that few of us choose our wives or husbands. Such choice is confined to arranged marriages where potential spouses are presented for inspection and subsequent choice. In the western world we do not *choose* our spouses.

**Few of us choose our wives or husbands.**

Marriage (or partnership) is an outcome that arises from a series of short-term choices. When we are attracted to another person we might choose to speak to him or her. But that is as far as it goes to begin with. At this stage we cannot predict the outcome of this first brief encounter let alone predict marriage, even if we desire it. It could be that this person is already married or has a partner. Having crossed the first hurdle to discover a free playing field and having established mutual interest we can then choose to arrange a date. Again the outcome of this date is not predictable. The hour or two together on the first date might reveal information that mitigates against future dates. We will never be sure until the outcome of that first date. Only then can we choose how next to behave. One thing leads to another. Eventually it might lead to marriage. More often than not a future marriage is 'presumed' after (but not before) 10,000 positive behavioural choices. This is the art of everyday choice, this is how we choose. It is not that we choose to get married to this particular person but rather that marriage is the result (or the outcome) of all these everyday choices. Choosing one small microbehaviour such as giving a particular look to a certain person can lead to a second microbehaviour such as some well-chosen words. This in turn leads to the choice of a whole series of microbehaviours. Ten thousand microbehaviours later we are married.

## Choosing jobs and careers

Similarly with the jobs we do. We rarely choose our jobs let alone our careers. What we do is make a series of choices that lead to the outcome of a job and career. It is not as if we set out, at the age of 18, to become financial director of a major airline or the senior partner in a well-known accountancy firm. We might find, as we go through school, that we are quite numerate and therefore choose to capitalize on this talent by choosing to study accountancy. But that is as far as it goes. What happens next depends on what newspapers and journals we choose to read, which job adverts to focus our eye upon and which applications we submit. The outcome is rarely guaranteed. It depends also upon whom we choose to seek and take advice. If we choose to take advice from the wrong person we might just be making the wrong choice. But we will not know until long after we have made the choice. That will be the outcome.

In making the choices in our lives there is little science but a lot of art. There is a lot of intuition and, hopefully, a lot of creativity. We have to create the opportunities and possibilities from which we choose. Such intuition and creativity has to be balanced by the negativity of the brain – whose sole purpose in life is to stop us making mistakes. If we have to choose between a good apple and a rotten apple it is the brain that is incredibly effective in helping us make this choice. The brain thrives on impersonal logic. It chooses the good by eliminating the bad. However, when it comes to per-

**The positive heart and the negative mind are always battling to achieve a precarious balance in life.**

sonal matters it flounders pathetically and often lets the heart take over, sometimes to good effect and other times to bad effect. The positive heart and the negative mind are always battling to achieve a precarious balance in life.

## Re-examining the choices we make

The aim of this book is to stimulate readers to re-examine the choices they make every day in life and especially as managers at work. The process of making choices is an art form, in fact our life and the outcome of our work is an art form. Where you are sitting now, the successes and failures you have experienced recently and your overall performance at work are not the result of scientific decision making but rather the result of your own artistic capability in creating your life and work.

**The process of making choices is an art form.**

You can choose to convert each written report you make into a work of art or into a routine piece of mechanical writing. You can choose to turn your next PowerPoint presentation into a work of art or just another boring half-hour talk. You can choose to make the next interview a work of art or a repetition of everything that has been said or asked before. Science yields a prescription in response to logical answers to logical questions while art offers a series of discoveries and new experiences that cannot be prescribed as a result of scientific endeavour.

## The art and science of choice

Science will never be able to produce the masterpieces of art that the likes of Shakespeare, Seurat and Shostakovitch have produced. The choice of each dramatic word, each brush stroke and each musical note is an art within an art. It is the art of application within the art of conceptualization. Work, management and business are no different. Art, in its broadest (but not conventional) sense is a key differentiator which impacts the success or failure of an organization. It is not all science. And it is not all scientific management. Without art a manager is severely limited to the rigours of the routine. It is the microbehaviours, the fine nuances of each individual word, of each brush stroke or of each note that differentiate the great masters from their crude imitators.

How you serve a cup of tea can be a work of art. To serve tea is the macro-behaviour. The nuances in how you serve tea are the microbehaviours. In Asia there is the ancient art of the tea ceremony. The total experience is more than serving tea but a product of the fine behavior that goes into serving the tea.

**How you serve a cup of tea can be a work of art.**

Any simple activity (such as serving tea) can become an art form. By choosing to make it so we choose to differentiate ourselves from the vast majority who adopt a run-of-the-mill approach and leave us uninspired and unimpressed.

Every single behaviour of ours can be a contribution to a work of art, to producing something special, to creating a great experience for others, to being different from the rest. However, we can only accomplish this greatness if we choose to put our minds to it, if we choose to create the fine nuances which will distinguish us from the crowd. It will be the unique choice of words that goes into a letter to a customer, it will be the choice of one or two positive strokes to sharpen or fade an image in a PowerPoint presentation, it will be the subtle and barely noticeable pause between two words when we are giving a talk, it is the choice of our microbehaviours that will determine the magnitude of our outcomes in life, that will enhance the prospect of great success.

It can be the way your frontline people accept a credit card at the counter and present it back (in Asia this is done respectfully with two hands). It can be the way you hand over money to customers if you work in a bank. One of my clients in West Africa carefully places the money in an envelope before respectfully handing the envelope to a customer.

## The choice of motivation

At a deeper level we have more profound choices, for example whether to be motivated or demotivated. Happiness is a choice. In my opinion there are enough things going wrong in this world for me to

**Happiness is a choice.**

choose to be continually unhappy. But I choose to be happy. I have a beautiful wife, wonderful children, an exciting job and a life rich with experience and learning opportunities.

## How to choose

The six chapters in Part 2 expand on the central thesis of this book. This is that 'our greatest successes are a reflection of our everyday choices'. The first two chapters examine what we mean by everyday choices and how these evolve into big decisions. The assertion that all choice is subjective and based on emotional influences is the subject of the next chapter and this is followed by an exploration of how we can harness randomness and luck to improve the effectiveness of our choices. The penultimate chapter of Part 2 looks at how most of our choices are based on positive–negative polarities while the last chapter focuses on the nature of microbehaviours in relation to macrobehaviours.

A practical method for putting the central thesis into practice is the subject of the three chapters that comprise Part 3. We look at the importance of hesitation, choosing outcomes and choosing to widen the way by using 'W-thinking' or wobbly thinking.

The last part of the book is a series of 22 short chapters that give a selection of applications of the 'how to choose' method.

The overall intention of this book is not to offer a prescription on how to choose but rather to stimulate readers to reconsider and expand on their approach to choosing with a view to achieving even greater successes in life and at work. This is learning HOW TO CHOOSE.

# PART TWO

# The thesis for 'How to choose'

## Contents

- Everyday choices
- The evolution of small choices
- All choice is emotional (and therefore subjective)
- The randomness of choice
- Choice polarities
- Microbehaviours

**The six chapters of part 2 compromise the central thesis of this book:**

**Chapter 2** *Everyday choices*
demonstrates that each one of us is the product of the total sum of all the choices we have made in life.

**Chapter 3** *The evolution from small choices to big decisions*
stresses the importance of microbehavioiurs and points out that a big decision is no more than an evolutionary culmination of small choices.

**Chapter 4** *All choice is emotional*
reveals that there is no such thing as pure, objective choice. All choices we make are subjective.

**Chapter 5** *The randomness of choice*
asserts that high performance is a function of randomness and points to a way in which random choices can be harnessed to increase effectiveness.

**Chapter 6** *Choosing polarities*
harnesses 'the binary code of emotions' to show that all our choices veer between a 'yes–no' or 'positive–negative' polarity.

**Chapter 7** *Microbehaviours*
differentiates between our high-level 'macrobehaviours' and the low-level 'microbehaviours'. It asserts that it is our choice of 'microbehaviours' that determines our success in life.

# CHAPTER TWO

# Everyday choices

## You are a product of all your choices

### Changing your choices to change yourself

You are not just what you eat or just what you think. The person you are is the total sum of all the choices you have made in life, including choosing to read this paragraph.

Should you wish to change yourself then you have to change your choices. This includes a multitude of small choices which you might well have neglected during your life. Similarly, if you wish to change other people you first have to change yourself by changing your choices.

Let us take a simple example. Imagine you have been manager of a department for five years. You are male and every day you come to the office wearing a tie. Day in and day out people see you wearing a tie. The only time they have seen you without a tie is at social events. The whole tradition in the organization is for men to wear ties.

Imagine what would happen at work tomorrow and for the next 20 working days if you chose NOT to wear a tie.

Under the spotlight of any pure logic this new behavioural choice would appear insignificant. Choosing whether or not to wear a tie to work is no different, under the scrutiny of logic, from choosing whether or not to wear cufflinks on your shirt, or one red sock and one yellow one, a leather patch on your elbows or a flower in your button hole.

**Your choice will make a great impact on your team and your business.**

However, I can guarantee that your choice (to be different by not wearing a tie) will make a great impact on your team and your business. Try it out, see what happens and please give me some feedback (my e-mail address is team@superboss.co.uk).

Conversely, if you normally come to work dressed casually and never wear a tie, try coming to work for each of the next 20 mornings wearing a smart suit and tie. Again, please let me know what happens.

The central thesis of this book is that the accumulation of these small behavioural choices (what I term as 'microbehaviours') has a major impact on our lives and work. As explained in Chapter 4 most things we do are driven by our subconscious. We thus tend to live and work in automatic mode. However, we can influence the course of our lives by increasing the number of conscious choices we make. In fact the default choice of not making a choice (by relying on the subconscious) will effectively determine our fate – by allowing our fate to be determined by others or by previously set routines, rather than by today's conscious choices.

## Conscious choices

All our conscious choices, and I am advocating more of them, accumulate to build up a pattern of what we choose to be in life. It is this pattern which influences the direction in which we are going, which determines how people see us and which leads to our successes or failures in life and at work. The better the grasp we have of our small everyday choices, the better the grasp we will have of the direction we wish to go in and the greater the probability that the outcomes we desire will be generated. Many of these choices relate to our microbehaviours.

**The better the grasp we have of our everyday small choices, the greater the probability the outcomes we desire will be generated.**

Box 2.1 is a list of 100 typical everyday choices relating to managerial microbehaviours which contribute to the influential pattern of who we are, what we want to be, where we want to go and what we want to achieve.

**BOX 2.1** Microbehaviours: Personal behavioural everyday choices

| | |
|---|---|
| **Choice 1** | What time we get up in the morning |
| **Choice 2** | Whether or not we eat breakfast (and what we eat for breakfast) |
| **Choice 3** | What we do while eating breakfast (chat to our family, listen to the radio, watch breakfast TV) |
| **Choice 4** | What news items we pay attention to on the radio or TV |
| **Choice 5** | What newspaper we buy every day (the same each day or a different one) |
| **Choice 6** | How much time we spend reading the newspaper |
| **Choice 7** | What we read in the newspaper |
| **Choice 8** | What we remember from reading the newspaper |
| **Choice 9** | What opinions we form as a result of what we read |
| **Choice 10** | What route we take to work (the same or different every day) |
| **Choice 11** | What we do en route to work (think, sing, listen to music, make calls, suck peppermints) |
| **Choice 12** | What we say (if anything) to the security guard on entering the building |
| **Choice 13** | What route we take through the building to our place of work |
| **Choice 14** | Who we talk to (if at all) en route to our place of work – and who we listen to |
| **Choice 15** | What we say when we talk to people and what we say when we listen to them |
| **Choice 16** | What tone of voice we use when talking to people and what face we put on when listening to them |
| **Choice 17** | How we genuinely feel about the people we talk to |
| **Choice 18** | Whether or not we ask questions and take an interest |
| **Choice 19** | Whether or not we seek opportunities to praise and celebrate successes |
| **Choice 20** | Whether or not we seek to compliment someone on something |
| **Choice 21** | Who we initiate conversation with throughout the day |
| **Choice 22** | Whether or not we really enjoy being with the people we meet |
| **Choice 23** | What we do immediately we arrive at our place of work (e.g. download our e-mail, make a call on our cellphone, chat to |

people in the vicinity, go through the in-tray, read the paper, listen to music, meditate)

**Choice 24** The gestures we adopt during the day (frowns, smiles, the look in our eyes, our gait, our hand movements and other gestures etc.)

**Choice 25** Which documents to bin, which documents to read and how to read them

**Choice 26** What outgoing telephone calls to make

**Choice 27** What inbound telephone calls to accept

**Choice 28** How long each telephone call lasts

**Choice 29** How much of each call should be chit-chat as opposed to business

**Choice 30** Whether or not to eat lunch

**Choice 31** Where to eat lunch

**Choice 32** Who to go to lunch with

**Choice 33** What to eat for lunch

**Choice34** What conversation we initiate over lunch

**Choice 35** What new ideas we come up with during the day

**Choice 36** What we do differently each day (as opposed to doing things the same)

**Choice 37** What initiatives we take during the day (e.g. ringing customers at random to find out how they are)

**Choice38** How much time we spend reflecting on recent events

**Choice 39** Whose advice we seek during the day

**Choice 40** Whether or not to take their advice

**Choice 41** Our response to unexpected events (e.g. a major customer complaint)

**Choice 42** Our response to interruptions

**Choice 43** Our behaviour with people we do not like

**Choice 44** Who we like

**Choice 45** What we like about people we meet

**Choice 46** What we dislike about people we meet

**Choice 47** What qualities we look for in the people we meet

**Choice 48** What qualities we look for in ourselves

**Choice 49** Who we criticize (if at all)

**Choice 50** How we criticize (up front or behind their back)

**Choice 51**    How we receive criticism from others

**Choice 52**    Who we solicit formal reports from during the day

**Choice 53**    How to reply to a letter (standard letter, personalized response written by ourselves or a response drafted by a subordinate)

**Choice 54**    Whether to inject some fun into the day and if so how

**Choice 55**    Whether to motivate our people today and if so how

**Choice 56**    How to schedule our time for the future

**Choice 57**    How much 'blank' time we keep in our schedule

**Choice 58**    How to use this 'blank' time (walk about, catch up on papers, go home early)

**Choice 59**    What topics we should focus our attention on today

**Choice 60**    What formal activities we should initiate over coming weeks and months

**Choice 61**    What training we and our teams require over the coming weeks and months

**Choice 62**    Whether or not to give some informal 'performance appraisal' feedback to people in our team today

**Choice 63**    What to communicate (and whether it should be formal or informal, face to face or otherwise)

**Choice 64**    How much time we should spend with our boss

**Choice 65**    Whether or not to attend a meeting we have reservations about

**Choice 66**    Whether or not we are happy

**Choice 67**    How we feel

**Choice 68**    What exercise we take during our breaks, during the evening or at weekends

**Choice 69**    Whether or not to call our spouse or partner during the day

**Choice 70**    Whether or not to keep a record of key events and 'happenings'

**Choice 71**    What new things to go and learn about

**Choice 72**    Whether or not to sit down or stand up when answering the phone

**Choice 73**    Which colour ink to use in our pen

**Choice 74**    Where our desk is and what is on our desk (e.g. photo of family etc.)

**Choice 75**    What to study during the day (if at all)

| | |
|---|---|
| **Choice 76** | How much time should we dedicate to studying during the day (or evening) |
| **Choice77** | What refreshments to have during the day (tea, coffee, cola or water) |
| **Choice 78** | How to welcome our guests (wait in the office or go to reception to greet them) |
| **Choice 79** | Whether to tap into the internet to check out the company's share price |
| **Choice 80** | Who to e-mail during the day |
| **Choice 81** | How often to check our e-mail |
| **Choice 82** | What to dream about during the day (our next vacation, golf at the weekend, the football match tonight or that person we really fancy) |
| **Choice 83** | Whether or not to have music playing in our office |
| **Choice 84** | How often we get up to stretch our legs |
| **Choice 85** | Whether or not we should chase something up |
| **Choice 86** | How often we should chase up something |
| **Choice 87** | Whether or not to support each proposal coming across our desk |
| **Choice 88** | What additional information we require before coming to any decision |
| **Choice 89** | What risks we take (e.g. what to authorize and what not to authorize) |
| **Choice 90** | How much time we put into people (as opposed to paperwork) |
| **Choice 91** | How visible we are as managers |
| **Choice 92** | How positive (or negative) we are as managers |
| **Choice 93** | What time to finish work and go home |
| **Choice 94** | Whether or not to take work home |
| **Choice 95** | What to say when we get home |
| **Choice 96** | What books we choose to read |
| **Choice 97** | What topics we want to learn about and become expert in |
| **Choice 98** | Who we smile at during the day, how we smile and the frequency of smiling |
| **Choice 99** | Whether or not to reflect on our day |
| **Choice 100** | How we reflect on our day (e.g. whether or not to record our random thoughts in an exercise book) |

It should be evident that this list of 100 choices merely scratches at the surface of our repertoire of choices. There are at least 1,000 other microbehavioural choices we could make. Each of these choices could be taken apart and subdivided into a further 100 microchoices. For example, Box 2.2 contains a further 26 choices relating to Choice 94 (whether or not to take work home).

| BOX 2.2 | Choice 94: Whether or not to take work home |
|---|---|

| | |
|---|---|
| **Choice94 A** | What work to take home |
| **Choice 94 B** | How much time to spend on working at home |
| **Choice 94 C** | Whether or not to ring colleagues to consult them on work being done at home |
| **Choice 94 D** | What papers to put aside |
| **Choice94 E** | What papers to concentrate on |
| **Choice94 F** | How to respond to each paper (e.g. respond by e-mail, call, face to face, annotation on paper etc.) |
| **Choice94 G** | Where to do the work at home (in the study, while watching TV etc.) |
| **Choice94 H** | How much time to dedicate to each item |
| **Choice 94 I** | Whether or not to read all of each document – or just to scan it |
| **Choice94 J** | How to prioritize the work for tomorrow |
| **Choice 94 K** | Whether to accept the figure work on the papers or check it |
| **Choice 94 L** | What questions to ask tomorrow as result of the work taken home |
| **Choice 94 M** | What further information to be sought tomorrow also as a result of this work |
| **Choice 94 N** | Whether or not to make some positive comments to the authors of the documents/reports taken home |
| **Choice 94 O** | Whether or not to start with a blank piece of paper in writing our own report |
| **Choice 94 P** | How much thinking time we give to each contentious issue |
| **Choice 94 Q** | Whether or not to jot down notes |
| **Choice 94 R** | Whether to make a decision now or leave it till tomorrow |
| **Choice 94 S** | How to respond to a feeling of tiredness |

| | |
|---|---|
| **Choice 94 T** | How to respond if our child interrupts us asking for help with homework |
| **Choice 94 U** | How to respond to telephone call interrupts (from friends or work colleagues) |
| **Choice 94 V** | Whether or not to work at all (or leave it till tomorrow) |
| **Choice 94 W** | What colour pen to use when marking up documents |
| **Choice 94 X** | What music to have playing while working at home |
| **Choice 94 Y** | How to feel about each item we read (and about the author of that item) |
| **Choice 94 Z** | Re-examine the point of all this work |

## Infinite choices

Our range of options from which to choose is infinite. In other words every day of our working life presents an infinite number of behavioural opportunities. The choices we make in relation to these will determine whether or not we will be in a job tomorrow, next year or in ten years' time. It will also determine what type of job we will be doing. The choice of questions we ask, the choice of people we talk to, the choice of people we consult, the choice of gestures we make, the choice of feelings we express will all determine our future fate. They will all aggregate into a pattern which defines a future outcome and a perception, if not definition, of who each one of us is as a person.

> **Every day of our working life presents an infinite number of behavioural opportunities from which to choose.**

With such an infinite range of options from which to choose it should be readily apparent that there can be no one simple scientific tool which effectively determines the best route to accomplishing a desired outcome. The permutations of personal choice are endless and any one person will invariably choose a different set of options from another. That is what makes us all different.

## The dangers of a prescriptive approach

While so many companies try to prescribe tasks and answers for their employees there is actually no effective prescription that can specify the exact microbehaviours which determine the fate of an organization. Yet so many companies try to be prescriptive in their approach. They believe that by developing procedures and rules they can eliminate choice and standardize the tasks and actions needed to achieve a specified objective. By attempting to eliminate behavioural choice they effectively regulate individual energy by channelling it down well-defined paths (or routines). Such direction is essential when, for example, flying an aeroplane, driving a car or completing an expense claim form. However, it does not work with the all-important interpersonal relationships on which all businesses thrive. That is why the prescription of a scripted welcome is so inept and inhuman.

**Regulations are no more than tools and it is our choice on how to use them.**

The delusion is that senior executives tend to believe that everything can be regulated by procedure and rules when in fact many of the key determinants of business success relate to the everyday behavioural choices employees make in HOW to operate these procedures and rules. Such regulations are no more than tools and it is our choice how to use them.

# The method of choice

The method of choice (effectively HOW to CHOOSE) is to create a conscious awareness of the extended range of options available to us and from which we can choose. To do this we need to hesitate momentarily before each impending behaviour and allow the intention to enter our consciousness for an evaluation of the potential outcomes of that behaviour and assess whether there is a more effective way. This is the 'HOW' method of choice.

**Nobody else can choose for us. Every single thing we do is OUR choice.**

Nobody else can choose for us. It will always be OUR choice no matter what advice, guidance or dictat we are given. When the self eventually awakens (normally during adolescence) there is a realization that, ultimately, nobody else can make a decision for us. Every single thing we do is OUR choice. We can go along 100 per cent with the suggestions of others but in the end it is our choice to do so.

Therefore to maximize whatever we wish to achieve for ourselves in life and at work we have to re-examine all these everyday choices with a view to expanding our range of potential options.

## Intellectual and emotional energy

This process of re-examining and re-evaluating our everyday choices requires immense reserves of intellectual and emotional energy. It is not easy. The easy thing to do is to repeat what we have always done before (and therefore to repeat our previous choices). This requires minimal energy. However, by pumping fresh energy into our method of choosing we revitalize our lives and our work experiences. We will effectively renew ourselves as individuals, replacing the worn-out and rutted grey cells of our 'old self' with fresh new matter in the brain, mind and heart.

**The easy thing to do is to repeat what we have always done before (and therefore to repeat our previous choices).**

Expressed another way, the more we rely on past choices (which effectively puts us into non-choosing, automatic mode) and the less energy we put into fresh new choices the more we allow ourselves to wither away on the vine of past experience. We die with our past choices and can only keep ourselves alive by energetically pursuing new exciting choices which will create a difference for our 'selves' and for others.

This means that we have to take off our ties when we normally wear ties. It means we need to speak to new people, ask different questions, create tough challenges, go on voyages of discovery, take risks and acquire new wisdom through everyday learning choices. Conversely, we must discard the tired old daily routines, break away from habits, challenge customs and conventions and become exciting new people as opposed to tiresome old nags.

The challenge is to become an even better person by, for example, changing the way we greet people, the way we listen to them, the way we compliment others – and the frequency with which we do so.

We cannot risk becoming a sculpture of ourselves. The aim should be to develop a dynamic living creation of our own personal art. Everything we do, every microscopic piece of behaviour is part of our performance on the stage of life, a performance watched deliberately or inadvertently by many more people than we think. The difference between the winner of the race and the one that comes in second is that microscopic piece of behaviour. When we concentrate on these microbehaviours and improve on them by choosing from a wider range of options we will differentiate ourselves from the masses. The people who make their marks are those who wear bow ties, cravats, colourful shirts when everyone else conforms to the uniform. One great cardiologist I know has long, flowing white hair and uses a fountain pen with red ink.

> **We cannot risk becoming a sculpture of ourselves. The aim should be to develop a dynamic living creation of our own personal art.**

It may be a self-evident truth (albeit a much ignored one) but by choosing to be different we choose not to be the same as everyone else. In doing so we choose not to follow the same old formula, not to replicate the path of convention and not to conform to the constraints of the prevailing mass. Progress in life comes from pushing back the boundaries and this starts with our choice of microbehaviours. It all leads on from there.

## Being different to be better vs 'village mentality'

Being different to be better becomes easy when we observe, learn from and challenge the conventions of others – with a view to becoming unconventional. If the convention is to go home and watch the soap then we should do something different: perhaps go home, read a serious book and learn from it. We should concentrate on moving forward rather than sticking to the status quo and the same old routines. The people who follow these are those most vulnerable to the tumultuous ups and downs of commercial endeavour.

To merge totally with the group and conform with all their norms simply confines us to their village. We choose to keep within the boundaries of their choices. We need to ask ourselves: 'Do we wish to stay in this village with the same people for the rest of our lives?' It is our choice. Do we want a 'village mentality' (known in the world of organizations as 'institutionalization') or something different?

When the village disappears (as many do) we will have no choice. That is when we are vulnerable. It is when the company folds, the organization gets reorganized – and when retrenchment asserts its negative arm. It is far better to prepare ourselves for survival in an increasingly hostile and competitive world by reflecting on our everyday choices and improving on them. Watching soap every evening and discussing it with our mates every morning will not help us too much with that. It might generate a positive outcome in the short term but risks a negative impact in the long term. The choice is ours. Do you want to be here or get there?

**It is far better to get somewhere where nobody has got before.**

All I know is that if we stay here too long someone will get at us and it will not be nice. It is far better to get somewhere where nobody has got before. Then everyone else will have the catching up to do. Why not be the best bus driver on Route 19 by choosing to drive better than everyone else and by choosing to be friendlier than everyone else? These choices will add up such that when Route 19 disappears you will be in the best position to find a new route. If I had a driver vacancy I would choose you in preference to the bus driver who chose to be the same as the rest – and did not even want to be the best.

## The choice opportunities

It is a cliché to say that life is full of opportunities. But it is, and most people do not even see it. They travel along the same old bus routes or train tracks and miss out on the many opportunities they could choose to seize every day. I call this 'I-thinking'. These opportunities are not big (like grabbing a million bucks) but are invariably small (like making eye contact with a stranger). It is the opportunity to smile down the telephone, the opportunity to drop by and see an old acquaintance, the opportunity to make your presentation to the board extra special, the opportunity to come in half an hour early to get ahead of the rest, the oppor-

**It is your choice to seize these everyday opportunities.**

tunity of going to visit a customer who has called you, the opportunity of personalizing a standard letter, the opportunity of dropping by to see your boss to give her some good news, the opportunity of taking your team across the road to Starbucks for a cappuccino or two. It is your choice to seize these everyday opportunities.

# CHAPTER THREE

# The evolution from small choices to big decisions

## We rarely make big decisions. It is our microbehaviours that determine our fate

### The evolution of choice from microbehaviours

Most so-called big decisions can be traced back through an evolution of very small choices relating to microbehaviours.

A big decision is just a figment of the imagination. It reflects a small choice we make at that moment following an evolutionary series of previously small choices. For example, we might consider buying a new expensive house to be a big decision. It is not. It is a small decision. We choose to feel dissatisfied with our current home, we choose to dream about a new home, we choose a location, we choose the specifications which appeal to us, we choose to examine our savings account, we choose to feel secure with the salary we currently earn, we choose to take out a mortgage, we choose to consult a financial adviser, we choose to look in the windows of realtors (estate agents). These are all microbehaviours. Then it is easy. We choose a new house. It is a simple emotional choice following an emotion we felt a few months before. It is not a big decision. It is the exercise of a simple emotion we have chosen for ourselves. If we knew we could not afford that house we would not have chosen that emotion, we would have put up with our lot and at worst chosen occasionally to moan about it.

**A big decision is just a figment of the imagination.**

It all starts with a choice of emotions about where we live. A large family I recently visited in Soweto in South Africa seemed perfectly happy with their small house with outside toilet. They knew they were far better off living in the Mofolo Township in Soweto than in the squalid shanty sprawl of Kliptown nearby. I suspect the immigrants living in Kliptown felt they were better off living there than in the poverty-stricken country further north from where they had come. The emotions we choose are relative to our current situation and our perception of it. To have our own hut with an outside toilet is therefore luxury when we previously had no home and no toilet at all.

It could be argued that a big decision is one that is likely to have a big impact on our lives. Certainly moving house does have a big impact. However, the outcome of a big impact is not necessarily the reflection of a big decision. A simple little error while driving a car can have potentially disastrous consequences, for example, a simple microbehaviour such as looking down to change a radio station and not looking at the oncoming traffic can cause a collision.

What we view as a big decision is effectively an accumulation of the small behavioural choices we make. These slowly emerge into a pattern which we fixate at one point in time and label as a big decision. It is not as if worker ants make a big decision to build a big anthill. Ants have virtually no brains and definitely no architects in their midst. As Steven Johnson explains in his book[1] ant communication is crude, typically possessing only ten or 20 different signs. Yet using these signs and thinking and acting locally their collective interaction produces global behaviour in the form of a mega-structure, an anthill.

## Big outcomes from small choices

Human beings have the greater ability to conceptualize a future event and therefore set goals. 'We will build an anthill' or 'We will build a Millennium Dome' (or a company called boo.com). However, the act of conceptualization (a microbehaviour) is but one small choice which emerges into a potential outcome through the actualization of many other small choices. If the outcome materializes then it can be viewed as big, but it is the evolution of a series of small choices that leads us there. In other words, all the small choices we make en route will determine the actualization of a potential outcome and this includes the original choice of what to conceptualize. Few people forecast that the Millennium Dome in London would be a failure or that boo.com would collapse within months of its launch.

## Random microbehaviours

In producing a plan to move from conceptualization to actualization it is virtually impossible to determine all the macro- and microbehaviours necessary to make it happen. The random behaviours that occur while implementing any plan will determine the outcome. Nobody planned for RailTrack in the UK to fail. It did, mainly because some unforeseen random microbehaviours meant a train came off the rails and caused a major accident. Nobody planned for Enron to collapse, or Swissair for that matter.

**In producing a plan to move from conceptualization to actualization it is virtually impossible to determine all the microbehaviours necessary to make it happen.**

What we view as big decisions are often undermined (or conversely enhanced) by such random macro- and microbehaviours. All big events can be traced to a series of small behavioural choices with randomness playing a major part in their eventual outcome.

Take Ford for example. In today's paper[2] I read that Jac Nasser, CEO of Ford, was fired last Monday by Bill Ford, the Chairman. To quote from the article: 'For months the Ford family was said to be unhappy with Jac's autocratic style and to be plotting to oust him.' These words are interesting. While things had been going wrong at Ford (for example, problems with tyres) it was the choice of an emotion (unhappiness) relating to choices of microbehaviours (leading to the perception of an autocratic style) that led to the decision (perceived as big) to oust the CEO. Big decisions are no more than an evolutionary product of a whole emerging set of macro- and microbehaviours – in this case the behaviours which emerged as Jac Nasser's style. It is these small behaviours that led to a major decision. The problem with tyres was an unforeseen random event which influenced the evolution of these behaviours.

Two pages later in the same paper there is an article[3] about Rod Eddington, CEO of British Airways. The subheading states, 'Despite huge job cuts, Rod

Eddington has struck a confident note in restructuring British Airways after the slump brought on by September 11th.' Again it is the choice of a microbehaviour in creating a 'confident note' that enhances the prospects of a satisfactory outcome following September 11. The actual decision to reduce the workforce by 7,000 and to withdraw 20 aircraft was a simple choice following some simple arithmetic (a huge drop in revenues at a time when costs and revenues were 'uncomfortably close to each other'). The future success of British Airways will depend not just on

**Big decisions are no more than an evolutionary product of a whole emerging set of microbehaviours.**

simple arithmetic (anyone could work that out) but on the personal behaviour (and thus choice of microbehaviours) of Rod Eddington and his senior team. It will be these personal behaviours in exercising the arithmetic that will determine success or failure, not the actual arithmetic itself. The unforeseen (and thus random) event that influenced this evolution of behaviours was September 11.

# A pattern of choices

I challenge any reader to give me an example of a so-called big decision that is actually NOT conditional on a whole set of evolutionary macro- and microbehaviours and random events. Everything perceived as big can be traced back to small things. The image on the screen of my PC here can be traced to 789504 pixels (1028 x 768) and the minor choice of each word and each tap on the keyboard. When I want to communicate an idea I am choosing a macrobehaviour. Microbehaviours are my choice of words for expressing this idea. When I have chosen the ideas I want to express together with 60,000 words these macro- and microbehaviours will, with any luck, emerge into what you and I describe as a book. A pattern emerges from all these small choices.

My choice in writing this book followed an idea that emerged in my head a few months ago. I then chose to ask my editor Rachael Stock for a meeting to discuss the idea. She chose to agree to that meeting. We chose to discuss the idea in a certain way and what evolved from that discussion was a modified idea. Rachael then chose to consult her colleagues and they then chose to offer me a contract which I chose to accept. From that evolved the book.

At that time September 11 had not happened, Jac Nasser had not been fired and Rod Eddington had not had to scale back on operations at British Airways. This book has evolved from a whole series of emerging events. It started with the microchoice of an idea and has been actualized through a series of other microchoices made by me and others. It is your choice whether or not to read it and learn from it. Everything we do can be related to such small choices and microbehaviours. At any one point in time we can fixate on a pattern of these choices and label them as a big decision.

## Strategic decisions

I have been a board director of a major company. A board likes to think it makes major strategic decisions. For example, a board might have to decide how many aeroplanes to purchase and whether to select Airbus or Boeing. These are not major decisions. They are based on a set of much smaller choices relating to financial arithmetic, specifications, commercial projections and past experience. The final choice also evolves out of previous choices we have made about the information we need to collect, the people we need to consult, the way we interpret information and overall how we feel. All these small choices add up to what appears to be a big decision.

**By the time the purchasing proposal reaches the board, the decision has effectively been made as a result of preceding microbehaviours.**

However, what appears to be a big decision is actually driven by these small choices. By the time the purchasing proposal reaches the board, the decision has effectively been made as a result of preceding macro- and microbehaviours. Most boards merely rubber stamp decisions. The small choice of 'rubber stamping' is a microbehaviour. It merely means saying 'yes' and putting your signature to a piece of paper. That is a microbehaviour, not a strategic decision. Similarly, if a board director protests against a proposed decision that protest is no more than a chosen microbehaviour. If another board director calls for more information, more time, or a second or third opinion these again are microbehaviours. Attending the board meeting and choosing to contribute are the macrobehaviours.

# Jack Welch

Many people acclaim Jack Welch as the most successful CEO ever. When he took over as CEO of General Electric in 1981 his vision was simple: to be a winning company of the future, to be number one or number two in the marketplace. That's a small choice. Each one of us wants to be number one in our own way; it is an emotional choice, it makes us feel good to be revered as the best. As he writes in his book:[4]

**"I came to the job without many of the external CEO skills. Our 500,000 plus shareholders had no idea who Jack Welch was. What I did know was what I wanted the company to 'feel' like. I knew it had to change... We have to permeate every mind in this company with an attitude, with an atmosphere that allows people – in fact, encourages people – to see things as they are, to deal with the way it is, not the way they wished it would be... This 'human element' would foster an environment where people would dare to try new things, where they would feel assured in knowing that 'only the limits of their creativity' and drive would be the ceiling on how far and how fast they would move."**

The success of General Electric with Jack Welch at the helm was due to this focus on the 'soft' microbehaviours that are so essential to long-term success. His quotation can be dissected in terms of the small choices that Jack Welch wanted people to make in aiming to become number one (Box 3.1).

| BOX 3.1 | Small choices and becoming number one |
| --- | --- |

**EXAMPLE 1**
*'I knew what I wanted the company to "feel" like'*
This is a choice of how Jack wanted people to feel. It is emotional

**EXAMPLE 2**
*'We have to permeate every mind with an attitude'*
Critical to sustained high performance is the choice of the attitudes which need to permeate through the company

## EXAMPLE 3

*'An atmosphere that allows people – in fact, encourages people – to see things as they are, to deal with the way it is, not the way they wished it would be'*

The choice of emotions and attitudes is then explained with some well-chosen words which describe a chosen 'atmosphere'

## EXAMPLE 4

*'This "human element" would foster an environment where people would dare to try new things, where they would feel assured in knowing that "only the limits of their creativity" and drive would be the ceiling on how far and how fast they would move'*

Here Jack chooses a set of macro- and microbehaviours, such as 'daring to try new things' which he would encourage

(Paradoxically, it was Jack Welch's 'microbehavioural' set of choices to form a close relationship with Suzy Wetlaufer, a journalist who came to interview him, that has created an outcome for him unforeseen when I started writing the above and what follows)

## Daring to trying new things

My 14-year-old daughter, Ruth-Elena, used to be scared of spiders. Yesterday she made a small choice. She confronted that fear and held a spider. The macrobehaviour was to confront her fear and the microbehaviour was actually to hold a spider. The outcome of this behaviour is the elimination of fear.

**'Daring to try new things' is volunteering for challenging projects.** 'Daring to try new things' is no different. It is stepping into the water when you cannot swim. It is speaking in public when you suffer from stage-fright. It is talking to a stranger or for that matter to the CEO. 'Daring to try new things' is volunteering for challenging projects; it is putting your head above the parapet to risk an unknown future consequence (for example, the risk of failure). All these are small everyday choices leading to microbehaviours which can lead to major changes in our lives.

Life is built out of these microbehaviours and General Electric was built out of the microbehaviours of Jack Welch's own conduct and the small choices he made, for example to focus on 'hugging winners'. The so-called big decisions fell out of this approach as a consequence of his emphasis on the soft side of management, as opposed to the more predominant concentration on hard issues (issues with big numbers that can be quantified in terms of dollars and cents).

## The issue of 'feel'

As Welch writes: 'To be a winner, we had to couple the "hard" central idea of being No.1 or No.2 in growth markets with intangible "soft" values to get the "feel" that would define our new culture.'

It is the small choices of microbehaviours that generate this feel, and it is this feel that underpins high performance and success. To be number one it is necessary to create the right feel. Should any part of your organization have the wrong feel then you are less likely to be number one.

The feel is reflected in microbehaviours such as a frown or a smile, in the tone of a boss's voice, in the way he or she communicates. It is reflected in how a boss devotes each minute of the day and each physical movement he or she makes. It is reflected in the words chosen to communicate and the emotions (or lack of emotions) that underpin these words. This feel all adds up to having a major impact on the organization, not only indirectly in terms of climate and culture but also directly in terms of the influence people have on decisions.

**To be number one it is necessary to create the right 'feel'. This arises from our choice of microbehaviors**

For example, the decision to expand a business by acquiring a new company is predicated on such soft issues as interpretation of data, attitude, experience and wisdom. These are all part of the feel and can only be addressed through making the appropriate choices of microbehaviours. The small choices of how much time to devote during the forthcoming week to the idea of an acquisition or to seek out opportunities or to analyze competitive data will lead to the emergence of a decision which will be perceived as big even though it is predicated on these earlier small choices.

If we do not look we do not see. It is our choice to look. If we do not see we do not get. It is our choice to see. There are so many opportunities in life which we do not see but others do.

# Reorganization: An evolutionary series of small choices

Another example relates to reorganization. New senior executives are often fond of restructuring the organizations of which they have just taken charge. This might be perceived as making a big decision with a big impact. However, such a decision is no more than a small choice relating to a series of emerging patterns in the new boss's mind. These patterns have evolved as a result of previously chosen microbehaviours.

Thus the choice to reorganize emerges from the following choice of microbehaviours:

1 The new boss chooses to interpret his past experience (about the ideal way an organization should work) in a certain way

2 He chooses to observe (or study) the new organization in certain ways

3. He chooses to see it in a certain light (he also chooses the light)

4 He chooses to ask questions

5 He chooses the people he asks questions of

6 He chooses whether or not to accept their answers

7 He chooses the information he wishes to obtain

8 He chooses his own interpretation of this information

9 He chooses to consult certain people

10 He chooses whether or not to listen to their advice

11 He chooses to devote so many minutes or hours a week to this issue

When he has made all these choices a pattern will emerge in his mind of the most effective way of structuring the new organization. It is then a relatively easy and small choice to determine the new shape. It is not a big decision, it is simply a decision he firms up on at 9.30 a.m. on a Wednesday morning. That is his choice, a small choice at that. The consequences of his choice might well be big, but his choice is no more than a consequence of all the preceding small choices he has made. That is evolution, that is emergence. The decision emerges out of a series of small choices.

# Big decisions are easy, small choices are difficult

Expressed another way, in life and at work it is the so-called big decisions that are relatively easy to make. The rationale behind such decisions drives executives through a series of small choices that virtually leads them to an automatic choice. It should be added that while so-called big decisions are easy from a rational standpoint, they often prove difficult from an emotional standpoint. This is because the emotional aspect involves an array of small choices relating to microbehaviours. It is these small choices that present our biggest and most difficult challenges. Using logic it is easy to make a 'big' decision to fire 7,000 people because of declining revenues. The real challenge and difficulty is an emotional one and relates to how we choose the microbehaviours to implement an easy rationale (firing 7,000 people because of a slump in revenues). It is thus the choice of microbehaviours that differentiates between success and failure. If you choose the wrong set of microbehaviours in implementing an 'easy' albeit negative decision you will make the situation worse rather than better.

**It is the small choices that present our biggest and most difficult challenges.**

What you do at 9.00 a.m. on a Monday morning will have a greater impact on your business than any major decision you think you are making that month. The two are, of course, related. Any major decision you make is a consequence of what you do at 9.00 a.m. on a Monday morning. Therefore you need to focus your energy on this. The major decisions will then fall out with such ease that you will realize that they are not major decisions at all, but simply small choices.

# The hard and soft side of business

The assertion in this chapter that there are no such things as big decisions, only an accumulation of small choices emerging into a pattern of events, might come as a shock to some people. This is because traditional management thinking has focused on task and targets as opposed to behaviour. It has focused on the hard side of business as opposed to the soft side. The hard side of business is easy. It is quantifiable, tangible and relatively impersonal. It is thus easy to focus on tasks and targets using systems to obtain the numbers and track the task. However, we delude ourselves if we believe that this emphasis will lead to our future success.

In front of me I have a textbook for students of business studies. It is a heavy large-format book with 553 pages, of which the last 23 are an index comprising approximately 1,800 references. A simple scan reveals that most of these index references relate to hard issues such as assets, balance sheets, best practice bench-marking or cost-based pricing. However, there are no index references to emotion, attitude, behaviour and,

**The 'hard' side of business is easy.**

values. Even the chapter on 'human resources' deals mainly with issues such as incentive schemes, selection techniques and application forms, training methods and performance appraisal systems. In other words, only about 5 per cent of the textbook covers soft issues and then nothing at all about individual managerial behaviour.

This textbook and much of modern management thinking and practice is a product of the scientific school of management which focuses on numbers, measures and systems as opposed to the soft side of emotions, attitudes, behaviour and the essence of those human relationships that lead to long-term business success.

## Managing tasks vs managing behaviour

By designating a person in an organization structure as a manager, he is led to believe that he is there to manage a team of people. In doing so he man-ages targets and tasks using numbers, measures and systems. The whole process of management becomes highly impersonal and is perceived as such. It is not deemed appropriate to 'manage behaviour' as behaviour is highly personal. However, it is behaviour that determines success, not tasks and targets which are a mere *product* of behaviour.

The most progressive executives today are those who concentrate much of their energies on this soft side of emotion, attitude and behaviour. That was why Jack Welch was so successful.

These executives focus on choosing microbehaviours that will positively energize the microbehaviours of others. In this way the tasks will be undertaken and the targets more likely to be met. Those who choose to ignore the impact of behaviour and focus solely on tasks, targets, numbers, measures and systems are those who are likely to fail.

A successful executive is one who is carefully choosing his own behaviours in relation to how everyone else behaves in the organization. When these behavioural choices are positive and effective, high performance follows and results are achieved. In other words, an essential precursor to any success is a focus on the behavioural choices of everyone involved in the organization.

## Automated decisions

Any business decision is no more than a behavioural choice – and a small choice at that. As soon as you attempt to automate decisions, for example as banks do with credit scoring, or insurance companies do with claims, then effectively there is no decision because there is no behavioural choice at that point in time. The behavioural choices were made earlier in the design and construction of the automated system.

The popular fashion for empowerment is no more than an assertion that employees can make behavioural choices when situations are presented to them. They have to choose rather than automatically follow the procedure or the manual.

**Any business decision is no more than a behavioural choice.**

Such choice is always emotional and relates to deep-seated feelings about what makes a person feel good or feel bad. Experience is a mere conduit to these emotions. It is experience that tells us what to do in a given situation to make us feel good. Experience is no more than an automated programme secreted in our subconscious which we can choose to draw on to direct our behaviour.

## Experience, energy and choice

We thus choose which experiences to remember as well as choosing our interpretations of these experiences. Experience is a set of tracks routed on a memory map. These tracks have been laid down as a **Experience is a set of** result of past learning. We therefore have to choose **tracks routed on** the route through these tracks of learning and thus **memory map.** choose the experience which guides us to a decision. The choice is deep and is vested in our emotions and feelings about what makes us feel good and bad.

Ultimately, these choices are reflected in our small behaviours. There is nothing else in life except these microbehaviours.

The biggest thing you will do today is expend a lot of energy. This might be physical energy (digging a large ditch), emotional energy (giving a passionate performance on stage), intellectual energy (completing the crossword) or spiritual energy (praying for people's souls). There is nothing bigger that you will do. Your day is no more than an accumulation of these expenditures of personal energies and such energies are very small relative to the energies of nature and the impersonal machinery of mankind's invention. The energy required of a pilot to fly an aircraft is infinitesimally small compared with the actual energy required of the fuel to put the plane in the air.

All behaviour does is discharge in a chosen direction very small parcels of personal energy, whether it be thinking energy (talking to oneself), communication energy (talking to others) or physical energy (walking among crowds). The biggest behaviour you will ever see is the star performance in a stadium and even that is the culmination of myriad previous small choices.

## The accumulation of small microbehaviours into patterns of success

To make progress in life and at work therefore we have minutely to study the small microbehaviours we make every minute of the day and how these accumulate into a pattern of events that we and others interpret as success.

This does not mean following a predetermined route but, in fact, exploring many different routes, many at random. It means experimenting continually throughout life with various microbehaviours to determine those that are more likely to be effective.

When we stop experimenting we effectively become trapped within ourselves, trapped within our own fixed rigid thinking patterns and the predictable behaviours that result. Such predictability makes us very vulnerable to the predation of competitors. Even behaviours based on morality and legality have to be challenged from time to time. I will leave it to your imagination for an illustration of what I am writing about, but today's morality can be yesterday's immorality – and vice versa to be honest.

# Institutionalization

Total reliance on tried and tested past behaviours is almost a predictor of failure. Look around you. You will see it everywhere. Everything changes all the time. It has to change to survive and if you do not change you will not survive. At best you will end up in an institution where everything is mind-numbingly predictable. Institutionalization is the outcome.

Thus, you have no option. You have to change and this means choosing to change, not the big things in your life (whatever they are) but choosing to change your own microbehaviours together with your thoughts and feelings.

**Total reliance on tried and tested past behaviours is almost a predictor of failure.**

### From September 11 2001 to nature and evolution

After September 11 2001 everything changed for me: I lost a lot of money; I had contracts cancelled; suddenly my predicted revenue stream decreased dramatically. Who was I to complain? I could continue the same old way and hope for the best. Or I could change. So I decided to change my approach, modify my services and the way I marketed them. After September 11 2001 the world changed and therefore I had to change too. That meant taking a few risks, thinking differently and behaving differently. It is too personal to go into detail but I am confident. If it does not work out then I will change again.

The secret of nature is its ability to adapt through change. Small changes are made in face of big changes. In turn, these small changes lead to big new patterns. Darwin called it evolution; the beaks on the birds became smaller or larger as the food supply changed – and eventually the birds evolved into different species. Change is a complex incremental accumulation of minute responses to evolving circumstances. Our behaviours are no different except that as human beings we are vested with hearts and souls from which we can apply emotional and spiritual energies to influence such microbehaviours. A daffodil has no such heart or soul and, further, it is arguable whether a chimpanzee does either. But definitely we do as human beings. Our choices derive from our hearts and souls. All choice is emotional and all choice is applicable only to our microbehaviours as a reflection of the way we choose to think and feel.

**Our choices derive from our hearts and souls.**

### Notes

**1** *Emergence* by Steven Johnson, Allen Lane–The Penguin Press, 2001

**2** Article by David Parsley and Garth Alexander, 'The dynasty that dumped Jac', *Sunday Times*, 4 November 2001

**3** Article by Robert Peston, 'Captain Calm flies through the storm', ibid

**4** *Jack* with John A. Byrne, Headline, 2001

# CHAPTER FOUR

# All choice is emotional (and therefore subjective)

## There is no such thing as a pure 'objective', 'rational' or 'logical' choice

## The difference between robots and human beings

Robots do not make choices for the simple reason that they have no emotions. No matter how sophisticated the robot every move it takes is a preprogrammed response to an external stimulus.

Conversely, as human beings, we are able to make choices because we have emotions which balance our reasons and vice versa. All our choices derive from emotions and are therefore subjective. If there is no emotional component to what we think of as a choice, it is not a choice at all but a preprogrammed response to an external stimulus.

In other words, there is no such thing as 'a totally objective choice'. We might pretend there is but the mask of objectivity we like to present merely hides the subjective influences on the choices we make every day.

Most of our behaviours, especially microbehaviours, are preprogrammed responses and contain no element of choice. Logic, rationality and objectivity at best moderate the emotions which influence our conscious choices in life. Reliance on logic alone would lead to the same decision a robot would make if it had the same software programmed into its brain.

**A mask of pretended objectivity merely hides the subjective influences upon our choices.**

**The logics we espouse are rooted in our subconscious programming, not in the emotions.**

Not only do robots have no heart or soul they have no consciousness either. They are therefore unable to make subjective choices. They are just programmed to react to stimuli. We are programmed to react too by way of the powerful but intricate mechanisms vested in our subconscious. Such preprogrammed subconscious reactions can only be overridden by a conscious process of choice powered by our emotions and moderated by reason. The logics we espouse are rooted in our subconscious programming, not in the emotions. In fact as revealed later we have to use emotions to choose our logics or rationales. Frequently, our reasons are no more than justifications for the emotions that drive our choices. The two influence each other: our emotions drive our reasoning while our reasoning can moderate our emotions. Any choice we make therefore includes an emotional component.

This applies to the way we choose our friends, business partners and what we do on a Saturday afternoon – there is always an emotional component to our choices, moderated (we hope!) by reason. However, it is the emotional component that plays the major and most powerful role.

Emotion is personal and emanates from the heart. It is this emotion that renders all choice subjective. Conversely, logic, rationale and reason are impersonal and therefore objective. In the same way that a robot cannot make a subjective choice (because it is programmed by logic to respond in a specific way and because it does not have a heart) a human being cannot make a purely (or 100 per cent) objective choice. When we arrive at a decision that appears to be totally objective it is because the preprogramming in our brains has followed a certain logic. There is no element of choice in this logic. It leads effectively to an automatic decision. The preprogramming in our brain producing these logics derives from the past learning experiences and knowledge vested in our memories and subconscious.

## Behaviours driven by the conscious and the subconscious

As we have said already, choice is a conscious process. It is difficult to imagine making a choice without being aware of the options from which we are choosing. Consequently, choice cannot be a subconscious process even though many of our behaviours (of which we are unaware) are driven by our subconscious. These 'automatic' behaviours are preprogrammed responses activated by various external and internal stimuli.

When we blink automatically no emotions are involved. However, when we wink at a child emotions are definitely involved. That wink is a conscious behavioural choice driven by emotions and moderated by reason. Both blinking and winking are microbehaviours.

It is worth exploring this assertion on a theoretical conceptual plane before illustrating it with some everyday examples.

## All choice is emotional: Theory

Let us assume we have to choose between Option A and Option B (see Figure 4.1). There are three reasons for choosing A and three different reasons for choosing B. Thus, while we choose B other people might choose A.

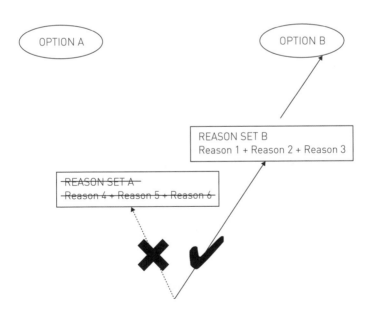

**Figure 4.1**  Choosing between Option A and Option B

We choose Option B because of Reason Set B (reasons 1, 2 and 3). However this begs two questions:

1 WHY did we choose these three reasons of Reason Set B (when the three different reasons of Reason Set A were available for choosing Option A – although we rejected these).

2 WHERE did this reasoning come from?

The reasons themselves were drawn out of our subconscious where they had been deposited as small segmented programmes of knowledge and experience learnt from the past, memorized and made available for future use. In this case we obviously *felt* that Reason Set B was stronger than Reason Set A.

The choice of Option B is, therefore, not based on reason or logic, but on how we *felt* about the two competing sets of reasons. This, therefore, is an emotional choice based on how we feel. In other words, we use emotions to choose our reasons.

If we attempted to use reason (or logic) alone, without drawing on our emotions, we would effectively eliminate the choice. There would be no case, no justification and therefore no reason for Option A (even given that this in itself is a reason for not choosing this option). Reason Set A would not exist and therefore our behaviour in choosing Option B would be automatic. There would be no other choice because there would be no other logic or reason. If Reason Set A does exist then we have to use emotion to choose between the two Reason Sets A and B. Thus all choice is emotional and therefore essentially subjective. It depends on how we *feel*.

## The binary code of emotion and 'emotional tags'

The feelings which drive our reasoning processes are directed by the 'binary code of emotion' in which we move towards what makes us feel good and move away from what makes us feel bad.

What we choose to do is tag our learnt experiences and thus our reasoning processes with emotions. It is the strength of this emotional tag (along the 'feel good ↔ feel bad spectrum') which determines our choice. We will feel better about one set of reasons (which we tag as 'feel good – positive') than another set (which we tag as 'feel bad – negative'). We will always choose sets of reasons which have a more 'positive–feel good' tag than another set which has a less positive or a negative tag

As stated already when there is no alternative set of reasons for making a choice we effectively have no choice. It is automatic. The reasons are completely sound and we feel very positive about them. We have no option but to behave this way. Therefore we have no choice.

**Choice only comes in when there are different sets of reasons from which to choose in reaching a decision.**

Choice only comes in when there are different sets of reasons from which to choose in reaching a decision. We then have to use emotion and feeling to differentiate between the first two sets of reasons (see Figure 4.2).

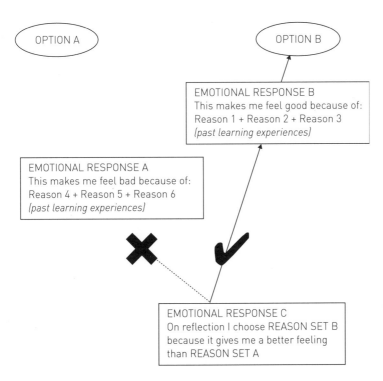

**Figure 4.2** Choice: Emotional responses

For example, let us assume that we need to appoint a new advertising agent and have to choose between two firms: A (Amber Associates) and B (Bright Board).

There are reasons for choosing either. The first set of reasons (1, 2 and 3) favours Bright Board while the second set of reasons (4, 5 and 6) favours Amber Associates. We thus need a third set of reasons and a substantial emotional component to enable us to make our choice (see Figure 4.3).

In this process we are choosing the reasons we like, because they make us feel good. Furthermore, we are pushing aside the reasons we like less, because they make us feel less good. The decision to select Bright Board might appear objective. However it is essentially *subjective* relying, as it does, on personal feelings.

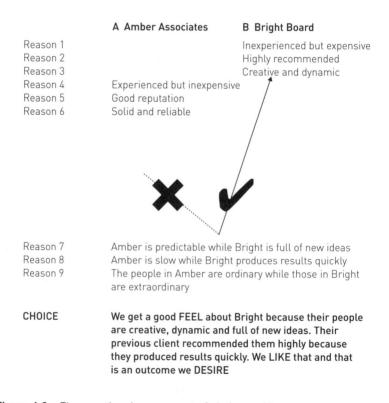

|  | **A Amber Associates** | **B Bright Board** |
|---|---|---|
| Reason 1 |  | Inexperienced but expensive |
| Reason 2 |  | Highly recommended |
| Reason 3 |  | Creative and dynamic |
| Reason 4 | Experienced but inexpensive |  |
| Reason 5 | Good reputation |  |
| Reason 6 | Solid and reliable |  |

| Reason 7 | Amber is predictable while Bright is full of new ideas |
| Reason 8 | Amber is slow while Bright produces results quickly |
| Reason 9 | The people in Amber are ordinary while those in Bright are extraordinary |

| CHOICE | We get a good FEEL about Bright because their people are creative, dynamic and full of new ideas. Their previous client recommended them highly because they produced results quickly. We LIKE that and that is an outcome we DESIRE |

**Figure 4.3**  The emotional component of choice making

This process of liking is totally emotional. It is about the way we feel about each prospective advertising agent, their qualities and what they bring to the assignment. It is also about the way we feel about our requirements for advertising. The whole process is subjective ('we feel good about this firm') even while it masquerades as being objective ('we have our reasons').

**Every choice we make is to do with feeling.**

Every choice we make is to do with feeling. We then justify our feelings with reasons as already indicated. The ultimate choice is thus based on the binary code of emotions. We move towards what makes us feel good (appointing Bright Board) and move away from what makes us feel bad (appointing Amber Associates).

In other words, all our choices can be traced back to emotions. We justify our emotions and feelings (and thus our choices) by explaining them with reasons and logic relating to past learning experiences.

At best reason and logic merely serve to moderate and explain our chosen emotions and resulting behaviours.

## The train tracks of reason

The best leaders rely on common sense or 'gut feel' to determine the choices they make. Sense and feeling are related. Sense and feeling generate emotions which drive us forward. We sense it is hot and move to a cooler area where we feel better. We feel this person is honest and are therefore prepared to trust him. Trust is a feeling. We *feel* trusted. It is not as if we 'think trusted'.

**The best leaders rely on common sense or 'gut feel' to determine the choices they make.**

It is not that reason or logic is bad, far from it. Reason is an essential tool that takes people from place A in their thinking to place B. However, the *choice* of place B is emotional. The use of reason or logic is essentially a train track that leads us to a desired destination, a place which will make us feel even better than where we are now. It is all emotional. It is emotion that drives us forward, determines where we want to be and therefore determines the choices we make in life. Logic and reason are just 'way-finder' directional tools, drawn from past experience and knowledge, that help us get to where we want. They provide us with the essential programmes that guide us to the outcomes we aspire to in life. In its moderating role reason helps us discard emotions that would drive us off course and replace them with more positive emotions that will keep us on course.

## Emotional conversion

Emotion and reason interact all the time with reason moderating our emotions and emotions influencing our reasons. Occasionally, we experience emotions (such as anger) that are so powerful there is a danger that they will drive us off course and generate a 'feel bad' outcome. Reason then intervenes to moderate the emotion and facilitate a conversion to a more positive emotion which leads to a 'feel good' outcome. This process of emotional conversion is illustrated in Figure 4.4.

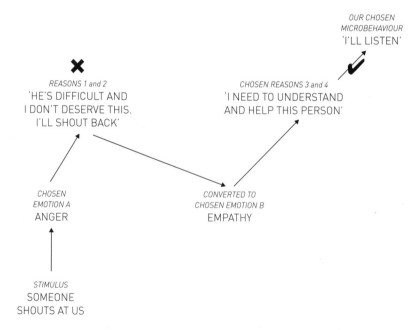

**Figure 4.4**   Choice: Emotional conversion (process)

In this way a manager can choose a different emotion to convert to a different and more effective microbehaviour and thus produce a more positive outcome.

When emotional conversion takes place there is an interplay between reason and emotion resulting in the choice of a different emotion to drive our microbehaviours. It happens when we sense that the emotion we are currently experiencing is going to drive us to a negative microbehaviour and an unsatisfactory outcome. We then choose a more positive emotion to create a more positive microbehaviour and outcome.

# Everyday examples

### Example 1: Choosing whether or not to smoke

A man who smokes will give you three good reasons why he smokes. Conversely, a woman who does not smoke will give you three good reasons why she does not smoke. The choice of whether or not to smoke is emotional, not rational.

All reasoning can be linked back to the emotions and the binary code of feeling good (positive) and feeling bad (negative). 'Smoking makes me feel good therefore I smoke. It helps me relax (reason 1), most of my closest friends smoke (reason 2) and my grandfather was a smoker and he lived to 87 (reason 3).' These three reasons are the justification for the feel good emotions he experiences when he smokes. In the light of such reasoning a smoker will resist the reasoning presented in the anti-smoking campaigns of the healthy-living brigades. The smoker is using feel good emotions to choose between different sets of reasons.

For a smoker to stop smoking what is required is more than reason – it needs emotional conversion. In itself the reasons to stop smoking are not enough. These reasons are readily available to everyone yet, despite them, many people continue to smoke. What is required is an inner conversion to an emotional state in which 'stopping smoking' makes a person feel better than 'smoking'.

## Example 2: A choice of candidates

While Example 1 relates to lifestyle the second relates to an essential management practice, that of selecting people for a vacancy.

In one of my previous books[1] I stated that, 'Subjectivity is essential when selecting the right candidate.' This flies in the face of contemporary business wisdom which attempts, but fails, to base all decision making on so-called 'scientific principles of management'.

The fashion is to use objective selection techniques to obtain information about candidates in judging their suitability for a specific job. However, the data collected merely serves to justify or at best moderate our feelings about each candidate, whether or not we like them.

**Selection for employment is an emotional choice in which rationality plays a subordinate role.**

Selection for employment is an emotional choice in which rationality plays a subordinate role. We all choose candidates based on our feelings about them. We *like* the fact they have all this experience, we *like* their positive approach, we *feel* we can trust them, we *feel* they will get on well with the current team, we *like* the new ideas they will bring to bear, their confidence makes us *feel* confident, we are *pleased* they have learnt so much about this new marketplace. We *like* the person, therefore we will offer him (or her) the job.

Our microbehaviours will be driven by these feelings and likings and will therefore determine the outcome of any selection process.

We recruit people we like and reject people we dislike. In the interests of objectivity and the law of equal opportunities we then hide our likings and feelings with a masquerade of reasoning. Instead of saying, 'I did not like the other person but I did like this one' we prefer to state, 'He fitted our profile better than the other shortlist candidate.' Subjective language is replaced with an illusory objective language. However, the choice is invariably subjective. Again the choice relates to microbehaviours.

Successful candidates strike up strong positive emotional connections with recruiters while failed candidates have less emotional impact and often inadvertently create negative emotional discords.

All other management choices can similarly be shown to be emotional, whether they relate to training, selecting suppliers, finding locations or choosing a marketing campaign.

# All choice is emotional: Lessons and applications

The key lesson for managers to draw from this is the importance of being in touch with their own emotions (as well as those of others) and understanding the influence these emotions bring to bear on all the choices we make at work as well as at home, especially in relation to our microbehaviours. When these emotional influences prove negative (e.g. malingering, whingeing, backbiting, non-cooperation, indifference and disinterest) the challenge for a manager is to stimulate a process of emotional conversion such that team members choose more positive behaviours (e.g. helpfulness, eagerness to please, open and honest communication).

**Successful managers need to strike a balance between emotion and reason, using logic to moderate emotions and vice versa.**

Thus, successful managers need to strike a balance between emotion and reason, using logic to moderate emotions and vice versa. That balance is pivotal in all the choices they make. It is a balance between heart and mind, between art and science. No successful manager can choose one without the other, although many attempt to do so.

# The three types of manager

This is illustrated in Figure 4.5 which shows the spectrum between a 'Type R' manager who is predominantly rational and a 'Type E' manager who is incredibly emotional, the ideal being a 'Type ER' manager who is well balanced.

It is worth saying a little about each of the three types of manager (Box 4.1).

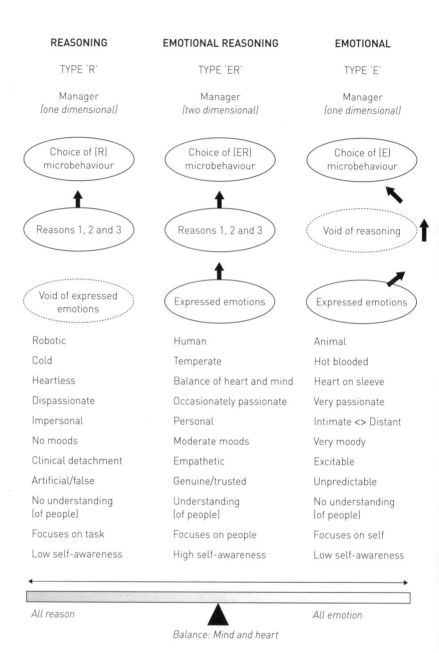

| REASONING | EMOTIONAL REASONING | EMOTIONAL |
|---|---|---|
| TYPE 'R' | TYPE 'ER' | TYPE 'E' |
| Manager (one dimensional) | Manager (two dimensional) | Manager (one dimensional) |
| Choice of (R) microbehaviour | Choice of (ER) microbehaviour | Choice of (E) microbehaviour |
| Reasons 1, 2 and 3 | Reasons 1, 2 and 3 | Void of reasoning |
| Void of expressed emotions | Expressed emotions | Expressed emotions |
| Robotic | Human | Animal |
| Cold | Temperate | Hot blooded |
| Heartless | Balance of heart and mind | Heart on sleeve |
| Dispassionate | Occasionately passionate | Very passionate |
| Impersonal | Personal | Intimate <> Distant |
| No moods | Moderate moods | Very moody |
| Clinical detachment | Empathetic | Excitable |
| Artificial/false | Genuine/trusted | Unpredictable |
| No understanding (of people) | Understanding (of people) | No understanding (of people) |
| Focuses on task | Focuses on people | Focuses on self |
| Low self-awareness | High self-awareness | Low self-awareness |

All reason      All emotion

Balance: Mind and heart

**Figure 4.5** Spectrum of choice

## BOX 4.1  Three types of manager

### The 'R' type manager

This type of manager relies solely on reason in coming to a decision. His emotions (if any) are suppressed beneath layers and layers of reasons which he relies on for all his communications and decision making. Because he never reveals his heart he comes across as cold but intelligent. His microbehaviours are fully programmed in advance. **He is effectively a robot.**

### The 'E' type manager

This type of manager subordinates reason in favour of allowing the full force of his emotions to drive his behaviours totally. His heart effectively rules his head. You cannot reason with this type of person. His reasons change from day to day and this makes him very unpredictable. His emotions are not moderated and he comes across as being far from reasonable. At times he can be wild, at other times sullen. His microbehaviours are not programmed in advance but are predominantly instinctive. **He is a dangerous animal.**

### The 'ER' type manager

This is the emotionally intelligent manager who is aware of his emotions and consciously moderates them to ensure that his behaviours not only reflect his emotions but are also within reason. He understands people and you can go to him for help. He is the type of person you can trust. When he communicates he does it with genuine feeling. Everything comes from his heart but with good reason. He has a good heart and a good brain. His microbehaviours are carefully considered and well balanced. **He is a people person.**

As a reader you might ask yourself two questions:

1  Where do I fit along the spectrum R <> ER <> E?

2  What type of manager do I choose to be?

If you choose to model yourself on an 'ER' type manager then your challenge is to establish a connection between your reasoning in coming to a decision and your genuine heartfelt emotions – and then allow this to show through in all your actions and communications. In other words, you must always strive to put feeling into what you say.

### Note

1  *What Customers Like About You* by David Freemantle, Nicholas Brealey Publishers, 1998

# CHAPTER FIVE

# The randomness of choice

## High performance is random

### Randomness, luck and high performance

High performance is a function of randomness. So is luck. The more you expose yourself to random opportunities at work, the luckier you will become and the higher your performance will be. The key theme in this chapter is that to perform well you have to create randomness of choice rather than restrict it.

If you select just one set of six numbers your chances of winning the lottery will be minimal; the probability is you will have little luck. However, if you randomly select 1,000 sets of six numbers then the probability is you will have more luck in winning.

Similarly, if you limit yourself to one tried and tested routine at work the probability is you will have little success. Conversely, if you go beyond the routine and expose yourself to 1,000 random improvement opportunities your chances of a win will be increased greatly.

One of England's greatest soccer stars, David Beckham, does not score with every free kick he takes at goal. In the match with Greece in which England qualified for the 2002 World Cup Finals he took eight free kicks. Only one, in the very last minute of the match, led to a goal. There could have been eight goals as a result of these free kicks; there could have been none. In fact there was only one. It was random. Furthermore, it was a random event that led to this goal, one of the Greek defenders fouling one of the English forwards.

**The more you expose yourself to random opportunities, the luckier you will become and the higher your performance will be.**

What makes soccer so exciting is that random events play a big part in the overall result, no matter how high performing each team is. The business of management is no different. By precluding random events no manager can win. Conversely, by exposing himself to random events there is an increased probability of succeeding.

Another example relates to a factory worker in Salford, England. In the evenings he used to sing Elvis Presley and Neil Diamond songs in working men's clubs. One night he was asked to sing something different, 'Nessun Dorma'. That one random request changed his life. The spotlight fell on him and two years later he has had two best-selling albums and is known across the world. He is Russell Watson. Another singing star, Andrea Bocelli, could also point to a random event that changed his life – when Pavarotti first heard him sing.

## The random illusion of success

Life is full of these turning points based on random events. In fact Nassim Nicholas Taleb, a trader in financial funds based in New York would assert[1] that: 'A large section of businessmen with outstanding track records will be no better than randomly thrown darts.' Winners tend to be visible while losers are given little attention. Thus if randomness throws up one successful CEO out of 1,000 we tend to focus on him rather than on the 999 who did less well. We then try to correlate his skills with success so that we can copy his skills. This is the same as saying: 'What are the skills that helped you win the lottery? – so that we can copy them.'

**Lif is full of turning points based on random events.**

The fashion for scientific management and the concomitant proliferation of rules, regulations, systems and procedures restricts randomness and the ability of any one individual to succeed. It leads to compliance and convention as opposed to challenge and creativity.

## Village mentality

For example, if you spend your whole life working and living in the same village, without setting foot outside it, the probability is that you will marry someone from that village. Should all villagers do this then the community will become inbred and die. Conversely, if you go beyond your village and travel the world the probability is that you will marry someone from outside your village and possibly from another country. Should everyone do this then all communities will thrive. The more random encounters you have with people outside your village, the more successful you will be.

**If you spend your whole life living in the same village, without setting foot outside it, the probability is that you will marry someone from that village.**

I am writing this on a Wednesday evening. Tomorrow I fly to South Africa to run two seminars. During my stays in Johannesburg and Cape Town I know that I will enjoy random encounters with people I do not know today because I have yet to meet them. Furthermore, I know that these random encounters will lead to long-term relationships which will be mutually beneficial. I do not know who I am going to meet but I do know that by putting myself around and chatting to as many people as I can in a room of 200 some positive good will come out of it.

I know this for a fact because there are some people I am scheduled to meet on this visit who I met, at random, on my last visit three months ago and with whom I now have a business relationship. They were chance encounters as a result of chance events. If I had kept myself to myself and just confined my South African connection to the one person who approached me six years ago I suspect I would not be visiting the country tomorrow.[2]

The chosen macrobehaviour of 'putting myself around' comprises a series of chosen microbehaviours relating to whom I initiate contact with and how I strike up conversations with people, as well as how I respond to people who initiate contact with me.

I mentioned Jack Welch in Chapter 3. Recently I attended an Institute of Directors' Conference at which Jack spoke. But I also went to network and meet people at random. I collected ten business cards and have at least three follow-up meetings scheduled as a result. There were 500 delegates in the room. I met ten of them at random. Something good will come out of this, not just for me but for the people I met too.

In attending this conference, I chose to sit next to people I did not know. I have a random technique for doing this. When the conference room was opened up I was one of the first to enter. I selected one of the many vacant seats and then waited to see who sat next to me. It would be a chance encounter. On this occasion the woman was American, we chatted briefly during the breaks and I will be meeting her in a couple of months' time to discuss business.

An alternative random technique is to be the *last* to enter the room. You are then forced to take one of the few seats remaining. Again this creates a random opportunity because you do not know who you will be sitting next to. This is the technique I used at the lunch table when I arrived late and could see only one seat left. The person I sat next to I am also due to meet soon to discuss business with. I did not know I would be sitting next to him, but now I know him. Much of life and work is like this.

The principle of random choice, as applied to choosing where to sit at a conference, is illustrated in Figure 5.1.

However, if you enter the conference room with colleagues and sit with them (and these are people you see most days) then you deny yourself the opportunity of random learning and creating beneficial relationships with new people (strangers) at random (see Figure 5.2). You are less likely to be

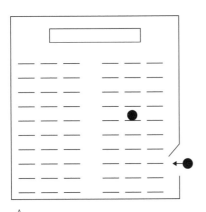

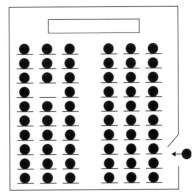

A
Be the first to sit down and see
who sits next to you

B
Be the last to sit down and find out
who you are sitting next to

**Figure 5.1** Random choice

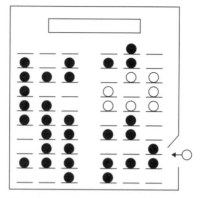

Sit next to people you know (shaded grey)

**Figure 5.2**  Limited choice

successful in the long term if you make these known choices as opposed to making unknown choices at random.

All these examples relate to microbehaviours and using randomness to drive them. By increasing the opportunities to meet people we can use random choice to increase the number of mutually beneficial relationships. In the world of business this must be more desirable than confining ourselves to the limited number of people we know.

## Random choices

Random choices can be applied to many of our everyday microbehaviours and many management situations.

Here are ten examples:

1  When attending a routine meeting sit at random next to anyone. Do not just sit next to the person you normally do

2  When attending a social gathering chat randomly to people you do not know, not just to people you do know

3  When attending a training event randomly select one or two people there and get to know them well

4  At lunchtime sit randomly at a table where people you do not know are sitting and strike up a conversation with them

5   Randomly select 20 customers you have not met before and invite them in for a glass of wine and canapés. Get to know them

6   Randomly select 20 people from your list of e-mail addresses and send them a positive message (e.g. a quote which appeals to you)

7   Randomly select 20 frontline employees who you do not often see and invite them to your office for a chat over coffee

8   Phone up 20 customers at random each week to find out how they are and how things are going

9   Go to a bookstore and randomly select any biography or autobiography, read it and draw from it at least one important management lesson. I guarantee you will find such a lesson

10  Select at random a name and telephone number from your company's internal telephone directory and phone this person on some pretence ('Can you just explain to me what goes on in your department? I'm very interested to know'). Get to know this person. You will be amazed at what you learn

## Unpredictability and the law of unintended consequences

Related closely to the randomness of choice is the principle of unpredictability and the law of unintended consequences.

As managers we like to comfort ourselves by believing that if we follow an established procedure the probability of success is higher than if we acted randomly without procedure. We like to believe that the successful outcome we desire is more likely to occur if we follow procedure than if we do not.

While procedure is essential in operating equipment (such as aeroplanes and trains) it is far from essential in dealing with people and managing relationships. Too much procedure in relationships can lead to customs and conventions which stifle creativity, minimize risks and therefore reduce the probability of success in a competitive world.

> **Too much procedure in relationships can lead to customs and conventions which stifle creativity, and reduce the probability of success in a competitive world.**

# 'Outward' choosing

When people talk about 'thinking outside the box', moving outside 'their comfort zones' or 'pushing back the boundaries' they are actually talking about stepping outside the customary procedures (for thinking and behaving) and taking the risk of seizing and creating random opportunities.

Instead of looking inwards at things and people we know 'thinking outside the box' means looking outwards at opportunities for learning about things and people we do not know. Every day presents at least 1,000 opportunities for such outward choosing.

Figure 5.3 illustrates this.

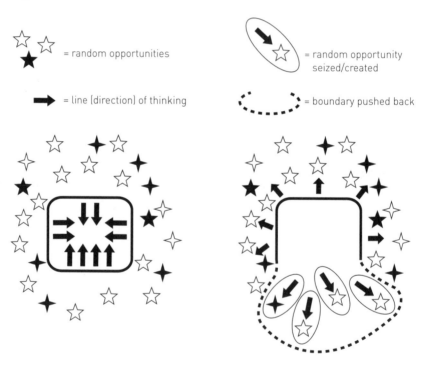

| INSIDE THE BOX | OUTSIDE THE BOX |
|---|---|
| Choosing to look inward | Choosing to look outwards |
| Choosing to ignore random opportunities | Choosing to seize random opportunities |
| Choosing to keep within the boundaries | Choosing to push back the boundaries |
| Choosing to follow procedure | Choosing to go beyond procedure, to take risks and be creative |

**Figure 5.3**  The randomness of choice: Thinking outside the box

By remaining inside the box we delude ourselves that we will accomplish the results we predict for ourselves. We ignore the fact that most of what happens in this world is unpredictable. For example, in recent times we have seen Swissair almost go out of business, the collapse of Enron, a massive decline in the fortunes of the reputable British retailer Marks & Spencer as well as phenomenal changes in the state of the world including September 11 2001 and a crisis in Argentina. A year before these events occurred I cannot recall a single pundit predicting them.

Our lives and therefore our work situations are much more unpredictable than we like to imagine. We make plans that are not accomplished and dream up visions that are rarely realized. Random events often overtake us and sometimes nearly overwhelm us.

What emerges from these random events is a different world. In the business community what emerges are different companies comprising people and managers  doing things in a different way. This difference, and the new world it represents, has been stimulated by random events, random encounters, random thoughts and random experiences. Thus the principle of unpredictability leads, through randomness, to the law of unintended consequences.

**Random events often overtake us and sometimes nearly overwhelm us.**

This principle and law is given little weight and therefore little credence in the world of business for the simple reason that senior executives, shareholders and employees seek the comfort of future certainty. This future certainty, described laboriously (and frequently monotonously) in strategic plans is merely an attempt to determine the future scientifically. Senior executives robotically troll through the steps they learnt at business school, blend in some personal experience with a touch of creativity and a huge dose of passion and hope they can achieve their vision of success. Randomness means that sometimes they do. But it also means that 130 companies (26 per cent) have disappeared from Fortune's list of the top 500 during the last ten years. Nobody planned it this way. Strategic decisions are made by the politicians, CEOs and leaders of this world the consequences of which are mostly unforeseen and therefore totally unpredictable.

If any investor had predicted the rapid demise of boo.com then they would not have invested millions in the company in the first place. Ernst Malmsten's book[3] provides a fascinating history of visions and predictions that never materialized. These visions and predictions were backed to the extent that the company was valued by investors at $390 million. It collapsed just six months after launching.

In other words, the consequences of a strategic decision, let alone a small behavioural one, are frequently random and frequently unpredictable.

A few days have passed since I wrote the preceeding paragraphs and I am now writing this in the British Airways Executive Lounge at Johannesburg Airport in South Africa. I am predicting that in a year's time British Airways will still be around as well this lounge too. However, the same prediction could have been made of Pan Am, TWA, Swissair and Sabena and a few other airlines a year before their fortunes collapsed.

As far as South Africa is concerned there were many people who predicted that it would disintegrate into chaos when apartheid ended. The reverse is true. It is now a thriving, vibrant country, forever improving and on an exciting road to recovering from its recent unlamented past.

## Exposure to random opportunities

The law of unpredictability is such that you can only increase the probability of meeting your predictions if you expose yourself to an increasing number of random events (encounters and experiences). In other words, your predictions are more likely to come true if you choose to move outside the box and expose yourself to the unknown rather than stay inside the box and rely on the known. This requires choosing a whole set of microbehaviours that are out of routine.

**You can only meet your predictions if you expose yourself to an increasing number of random events (encounters and experiences).**

The paradox is that seizing the unknown at random is more likely to realize your predictions than relying on the known. Companies and individuals that remain in the box and block out randomness are much less likely to achieve the success they predict for themselves, whereas those that expose themselves to the risk of the unknown and the random consequences this brings are more likely to accomplish their prediction of success.

Thus, if you send a mailshot to 10,000 people you might be able to forecast that 2 per cent will respond and you will receive 200 orders. However, it is impossible to forecast which 200 people will respond. These orders will arise at random. Should you have been able to forecast who these 200 people were then you would have sent out only 200 mailshots and saved yourself a lot of money.

## An analogy with nature

There is an analogy with nature in the theory and practice of randomness. Animals and plants readily adapt when they are exposed to random changes in the environment. That is evolution. Similarly, companies and individuals that energetically expose themselves to the randomness of external events are more likely to adapt and evolve successfully than those that shut the lid on the box and seek the protection of the known. The lack of random stimuli will cause them to shrivel up and die.

In practice this means 'doing things at random and seeing what happens' as opposed to 'doing predetermined things and expecting something to happen'. It means undertaking experiments, taking risks and doing the opposite of what everyone (especially your competitors) should be doing. It means flying economy when you normally fly business class, it means doing the opposite of what your merchandising manager says and experimenting at random with different types of window displays, it means randomly selecting a price as opposed to calculating it and it means random marketing initiatives. This flies in the face of convention even though it is totally predictable that some of the most successful companies today (such as Ryanair, EasyJet and Virgin) have flown in the face of convention.

> It means doing things at random and 'seeing what happens' as opposed to doing predetermined things and 'expecting something to happen'.

The risks are high and there is no guarantee of success if you choose to expand the randomness of your approach. However, there is an increased probability of failure should you restrict yourself to tried and tested ways which preclude randomness.

### Encouraging people to 'chance' upon improvements

You must encourage your employees to think in random ways and thereby to 'chance' on improvements to your business. You must encourage your salespeople to engage with customers in random ways and thereby chance on increased sales. Do not stand behind the counter (that is, inside the box). Go round the front of the counter and randomly engage customers. Do not wait for customers to call you. Call them at random. Discuss anything at random. Choose a colour at random and experiment with that; try not to be too scientific in choosing anything.

The *underlying principle* in this chapter is that you should harness the randomness of the external world to your advantage by expanding the range of options presenting themselves to you and choose from this expanded range at random.

The principle of unpredictability and the law of unintended consequences is more likely to fall in your favour by doing so than if you restrict yourself to a much narrower range of known opportunities. In other words, do not confine yourself to choosing between Options A and B because you know a lot about each, but expose yourself to Options A, B... Z, even if you do not know much about X, Y and Z. For example, when selecting candidates for a vacancy do not rely on the predictable stereotypes who conform to that boring old person specification but go looking for candidates who do not conform. Take a risk. It might not pay off but by acting at random there is an increased probability it will.

## Two qualifications

Having advocated that you choose from an increasingly random set of options it is important to add two qualifications.

### Organic vs inorganic situations

The principle of unpredictability and the law of unintended consequences is only relevant in organic situations. With inorganic situations science is well able to predict the consequences of a force acting upon an object. Thus we can predict that a glass window will break when we throw a stone at it.

What we are less able to predict is who will throw a stone and when. Business is built on organic relationships, not on impersonal inorganic scientific situations. We can predict that the new office block will be built within two years but we are less able to predict the occupancy levels and the relationships various companies will have with the landlord.

## Common sense

Common sense must be used to moderate the use of randomness in making our choices. If we know for sure it will NOT work then it is only an idiot that will attempt to make it work. Thus by increasing the range of options from which to choose we should never attempt to include options which we know for sure will NOT work. Choosing options from outside the box does not mean ignoring the knowledge and wisdom that is within the box. However, this knowledge and wisdom must be challenged from time to time. The world is not flat and despite what everyone believed (and no one predicted) it was possible to destroy the twin towers of the World Trade Center simultaneously.

Expressed another way: If we know for sure it is impossible then we should not attempt it. What we should do is increase the range of options from which to choose in creating desired outcomes. We should focus on the possibilities that arise from the increasing number of random options as opposed to attempting to convert an impossible option into a possibility. In other words, do not approach me at random and invite me to fly the aeroplane. However, if you are an airline company seeking trainee pilots then it is possible that there is an extended range of options from which you can randomly choose as opposed to relying on the conventional routes.

**What we should do is increase the range of options from which to choose in creating desired outcomes.**

The prime focus of this book is behavioural choice. The assertion in this chapter is that your success in business and at work is more likely to occur by using randomness to expand your range of behavioural choices (especially your choices of microbehaviours) and thus your network of relationships both within the company and externally. Most successful businesspeople have an extensive network of relationships. Such networks are built at random by exposure to a large number of people in a variety of settings. Should you close the door of your office it is less likely that that all-important person will walk in than if you keep it open.

## Corollary

As a corollary to this chapter, I have just returned from South Africa. Before the flight took off I chose to change my seat, moving back one row where there was a space between my aisle seat and the guy on the other aisle.

I chose to chat to him. His name was Dave. He hailed from Inverness in Scotland. He used to be a printer. Eight years ago his employer went bankrupt. There were no jobs available in the printing industry and Dave became unemployed. He chose to take a government-sponsored retraining course in microelectronics and robotics. At the end of the course he sent his career resumé to 20 different companies and picked up a local job as an electrical engineer. Nine months later he was approached by one of the other companies he had sent his resumé to. It was an oil exploration company and they were looking for an underwater photographer who understood robotics. He took the job, was trained up and now travels the world working on oil rigs and exploration vessels. He loves his job, is paid exceptionally well and has travelled the world visiting a wide range of exotic locations.

Dave did not seek out this job. However, he did choose to extend his range of options by circulating his resumé to 20 different companies. It was a random choice that precipitated him into a great job he had not even dreamt of before.

## Notes

1 *Fooled by Randomness* by Nassim Nicholas Taleb, Texere, 2001
2 Two months later, as I edit this chapter, my prediction of some positive random encounters has come true. I return to Cape Town soon to undertake a programme of work initiated as a result of one of these random encounters
3 *boo hoo* by Ernst Malmsten, Random House, 2001

CHAPTER SIX

# Choosing polarities

## Always choose the positive polarity

## The 'yes' or 'no' polarity

As mentioned in previous chapters most of what we do is determined by subconscious forces. It is not as if we instruct each of our legs to move when we walk. We just walk. We do not even think whether it should be the left foot or right foot that should go forward next. Most times we do not even thinking about breathing. We just breathe.

Choice arises when we raise potential activities to conscious level and say 'yes' or 'no' to each potential activity. We might feel like slapping our child but then we make a conscious 'yes' or 'no' choice.

**All choices we make are based on simple polarities equivalent to a 'yes' or 'no' decision.**

In fact, all the choices we make in life are based on simple polarities equivalent to a 'yes' or 'no' decision. These polarities relate to the 'binary code of emotions' that creates our basic motivational drives. Summarily, this binary code states that:

1  We move towards what makes us feel good

2  We move away from what makes us feel bad

All our activities can be traced back to this binary code. There is no exception. Nobody sets out to make themselves feel bad. Even those people who inflict pain on themselves do it because they mistakenly believe it will make them feel better ('the world will love me more if I become a victim').

Choice is therefore all about elevating potential microbehaviours from the subconscious (where they would be activated automatically) to the conscious (where hesitation allows a process of deliberation before activation).

This all-important process of deliberation enables us to choose the most appropriate macro- and microbehaviour given the chosen rationale (or reason or logic). We see the child behaving badly and instead of instinctively (or automatically) striking out at the kid, we hesitate, deliberate and then choose 'yes' or 'no' in relation to the potential activity of slapping him. In Chapter 4 I have described this as 'emotional conversion'.

As stated earlier this 'yes' or 'no' choice is determined by our binary code of emotions. What will make us feel good in the circumstances? What will make us feel bad in the circumstances? Our feelings or emotions drive our behaviours which we then justify with logic ('the kid was behaving so badly I had no option but to slap him – to teach him a lesson'). The mother momentarily feels good. She has taught her son a lesson by slapping him. Another mother might realize that slapping her son will actually make HER feel bad. Afterwards she will feel guilty and suffer a degree of remorse for inflicting pain on her son. So she chooses not to smack her son, preferring perhaps to distract him with another activity which will make him feel better as well as her.

## Expanding our range of polarities

To become more effective in making these 'yes' or 'no' choices about potential activities we need to develop ourselves by expanding the range of polarities which will form the basis of our choice. Wise people have a much wider range of polarities available to them than the unwise. As a result, wise people can choose from a wider range of potential behaviours to address any situation.

Choosing between 'yes' and 'no' polarities can also be applied to any management situation, whether it be dealing with employees who underperform or customers who are being abusive. The choice of polarities also relates to the minutiae of our behaviours (or what I describe as microbehaviours). Examples of these are the nuances we use when talking with people and the gestures we make when with them.

Box 6.1 gives just a few examples of the 'yes/no' polarities that can form the basis of our choices. They all relate to the binary code of 'feeling good' vs 'feeling bad'.

**BOX 6.1** Choice polarities

| Yes/No? | | Yes?/No? | |
|---|---|---|---|
| **Positive or negative?** | | **Positive or negative?** | |
| New | Old | Fresh | Stale |
| Healthy | Unhealthy | Interesting | Uninteresting |
| Easy | Difficult | Nice | Nasty |
| Helpful | Unhelpful | Giving | Taking |
| Unselfish | Selfish | Soft | Hard |
| Light | Dark | Open | Closed |
| Honest | Dishonest | Genuine | False |
| Trustworthy | Not trustworthy | Clean | Dirty |
| Flexible | Rigid | Controlled | Uncontrolled |
| Limited | Unlimited | Friendly | Unfriendly |
| Enthusiastic | Unenthusiastic | Caring | Uncaring |
| (Bottom) up | (Top) down | For | Against |
| Praise | Criticism | Together | Separate |
| Independent | Dependent | High risk | Low risk |
| Safe | Dangerous | Strength | Weakness |
| Opportunity | Threat | Friend | Enemy |
| Go | Stop | Fast | Slow |
| Warm | Chilly | Valued | Not valued |
| Understood | Misunderstood | Beautiful | Ugly |
| Supported | Unsupported | Knowledge | Ignorance |
| Wise | Foolish | Like | Dislike |
| Love | Hate | Experienced | Inexperienced |
| Mature | Immature | Valued | Devalued |
| etc. | etc. | etc. | etc. |

The examples in the box are just a few of the many polarities that can be used to form the basis of our choice. In a management situation we need to ask ourselves: What are the 'yes/no' polarities that will form the basis of our choice in creating the following outcomes:

1  We feel good?

2  Others feel good? (others being customers, employees, company executives, shareholders etc.)

For example, we can use these polarities in choosing our microbehaviours in response to a complaint from a customer. The 'opportunity–threat' polarity is one such example. We can choose to see the complaint as an opportunity or a threat and this in turn will determine our choice of microbehaviour. The 'supported–unsupported' polarity would be another example. We can choose a response to the complaint which leads to an outcome in which the customer feels supported (as opposed to unsupported – the cause of the complaint).

Another example might relate to a manager who observes a new employee attempting something difficult but 'is not doing it quite right'. The manager is unsure how he should handle the situation. Should he appear negative and criticize this new employee? Using choice polarities he can modify his microbehaviours as indicated in Figure 6.1 which illustrates some of the polarities available to this manager.

These specific polarities, driven by the binary code of emotions, are linked to our chosen set of values (being genuine, being helpful, being open, being honest, being caring etc.).

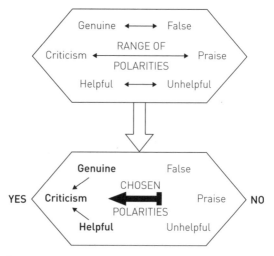

**Figure 6.1**  Range of polarities available

# Using polarities to make more positive choices

By thinking in terms of polarities we can make different choices if we find ourselves veering to a negative decision. In the case we just examined the cited polarities could be used to make a more effective positive choice.

Thus why not praise the new employee for attempting something difficult and then suggest an improvement? In this way direct criticism could be avoided (see Figure 6.2).

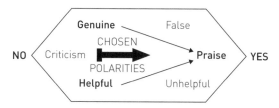

**Figure 6.2** Using polarities to make positive choices

# Polarities and customer choice

Customers also make choices based on these polarities. For example, if we walk into a café we will tend to use the 'clean–dirty' polarity to select one of the clean tables available – and avoid a table that is cluttered with dirty plates and debris. However, by reviewing and changing the polarities a completely different choice could be made. Thus why not move toward a dirty table and clean it ourselves? This would mean choosing the positive from a different polarity, that of 'helpful/unhelpful'. With this choice we would help the busy waiters and waitresses. Why not help people – even waiters and waitresses? The answer lies in the polarities we choose. In this case we substitute a negative polarity (we move away from a 'dirty' table) with a positive one (we 'help' by cleaning the table).

Box 6.2 contains some further examples of choice polarities applied to management situations. Each example shows an initial choice polarity followed by a reconsidered choice polarity. The CHOICE is highlighted in bold letters. The need for deliberation (or hesitation) is paramount in reconsidering the choice polarities and therefore making more effective choices.

## BOX 6.2 More choice polarities

**1** Selecting a person to be a personal assistant

| INITIAL CHOICE POLARITIES | | ➠ | RECONSIDERED CHOICE POLARITIES | |
|---|---|---|---|---|
| *Yes* | *No* | ➠ | *Yes* | *No* |
| **Beautiful** | Ugly | ➠ | **Hardworking** | Lazy |
| **Young** | Old | ➠ | **Trustworthy** | Untrustworthy |
| **Friendly** | Unfriendly | ➠ | **Friendly** | Unfriendly |
| **Intelligent** | Unintelligent | ➠ | **Wise** | Ignorant |
| **Experienced** | Inexperienced | ➠ | **Open-minded** | Close-minded |

*(initial and reconsidered choices are in **bold**)*

**2** Responding to an interruption

| INITIAL CHOICE POLARITIES | | ➠ | RECONSIDERED CHOICE POLARITIES | |
|---|---|---|---|---|
| *Positive* | *Negative* | ➠ | *Positive* | *Negative* |
| Smile | **Frown** | ➠ | **Smile** | Frown |
| Accept | **Resist** | ➠ | **Accept** | Resist |
| Friendly | **Unfriendly** | ➠ | **Friendly** | Unfriendly |
| Giving (time) | **Taking (time)** | ➠ | **Giving (time)** | Taking (time) |
| Easy | **Difficult** | ➠ | **Easy** | Difficult |

**3** Responding to a request for a roster change

| INITIAL CHOICE POLARITIES | | ➠ | RECONSIDERED CHOICE POLARITIES | |
|---|---|---|---|---|
| *Yes* | *No* | ➠ | *Yes* | *No* |
| Flexible | **Rigid** | ➠ | **Flexible** | Rigid |
| Unselfish | **Selfish** | ➠ | **Encouraging** | Discouraging |
| For | **Against** | ➠ | **Empowering** | Controlling |
| Agree(able) | **Disagree(able)** | ➠ | **Agree(able)** | Disagree(able) |
| Easy | **Difficult** | ➠ | **Interested** | Disinterested |

**4** Choosing whether or not to volunteer for tough project

| INITIAL CHOICE POLARITIES | | ➠ | RECONSIDERED CHOICE POLARITIES | |
|---|---|---|---|---|
| *Yes* | *No* | ➠ | *Yes* | *No* |
| Easy | **Difficult** | ➠ | **Difficult** | Easy |
| Experienced | **Inexperienced** | ➠ | **Inexperienced** | Experienced |
| Strength | **Weakness** | ➠ | **Strength** | Weakness |

| Enthusiastic | **Unenthusiastic** | ⏩ | **Enthusiastic** | Unenthusiastic |
|---|---|---|---|---|
| Low risk | **High risk** | ⏩ | **High risk** | Low risk |

**5** Choosing whether to confront a difficult person

| INITIAL CHOICE POLARITIES | | ⏩ | RECONSIDERED CHOICE POLARITIES | |
|---|---|---|---|---|
| *Yes* | *No* | ⏩ | *Yes* | *No* |
| Face up to | **Avoid** | ⏩ | **Face up to** | Avoid |
| Safe | **Dangerous** | ⏩ | **Courage** | Cowardly |
| Open | **Closed** | ⏩ | **Open** | Closed |
| Praise | **Criticism** | ⏩ | **Genuine** | False |
| For (person) | **Against (person)** | ⏩ | **Be helpful** | Be unhelpful |

By putting our choices into the context of these 'YES/NO' polarities we effectively broaden our range of options and thus create opportunities to be more effective. To do so requires deliberation through 'hesitation'. Many of our initial choices (as indicated in the bold in the left-hand column of the box) are instinctive. They lack consideration.

## Choosing to say 'yes'

The process of deliberation (through hesitation) enables us to bring other factors into play. It also provides us with conscious thinking time to consider additional options – for example, saying 'yes'.

For many managers the biggest struggle they have is to say 'yes'. They have been brought up to say 'no' (because most people have said 'no' to them in the past) and therefore they feel uneasy saying 'yes'.

**For many managers the biggest struggle they have is to say 'yes'.**

'Yes' is a choice, the other options being 'no', 'perhaps', 'another time', 'we'll see', 'I'm not sure' or 'not today'. Many managers prefer these other choice options. Each of these options is a microbehaviour.

Londoner Simon Tupman, now based in Australia, tells a story of how his 81-year-old mother buys a loaf of her favourite bread from a baker in Blackheath. She used to slice it herself but when her hands became arthritic she had to ask the baker to help her. He willingly obliged and sliced her bread. On one of his visits to see his mother Simon went to buy his mother her favourite loaf. The baker told him that the slicing machine had broken down. Simon said, 'Don't worry' and bought the loaf anyway. On his walk back he passed a second baker. With much forethought, great determination as well as with immense trepidation he took the loaf purchased from the first baker into the second baker and asked if he would slice it for him, explaining that the other baker's slicer wasn't working.

The assistants in the second baker laughed him out of the shop. 'You must be joking!' they said as they refused to slice the other baker's loaf. Back home Simon told his 81-year-old mother the story. 'Simon,' she said, 'you're crazy, you were wasting your time, nobody goes to that second baker.'

**Whenever you are inclined to say 'no', hesitate, think carefully and then switch your heart and mind back to the positive 'yes' polarity.**

Whenever you are inclined to say 'no', hesitate, think carefully and then switch your heart and mind back to the positive 'yes' polarity. Slice the bread. The long-term dividends will be phenomenal. Choose to be positive. Always.

Being positive, saying 'yes' whenever possible is the ultimate choice polarity.

## The negative polarity of self-protection

Self-protection is invariably negative. We like to say 'no' to prevent ourselves succumbing to the things we do not like in life, such as too much work, extra effort without reward or making sacrifices in favour of others – especially those who appear not to appreciate it. We encapsulate ourselves within this invisible shell of negativity – although with age the shell becomes increasingly visible: we become grumpy, difficult, irritable, prickly and frequently wear a frown on our forehead. Our words are sprinkled with negative phrases like, 'can't do that', 'don't like that', 'you must be joking', 'no way', 'it's not on', 'can't afford that', 'I don't agree', 'don't do that', 'I'm not sure about that', 'the problem is...', or simply 'no!'. We look fierce, tense, grim or miserable and others frequently think that we are 'in a mood'. The microbehaviours we choose will emanate from this shell of negativity.

Negative managers find everything too difficult. They do not like the risks of stepping out of the shell and venturing into the unknown. They conform to the negative 'mustn't do that' regulations of the company and hide behind these as an excuse for doing nothing else. Negative managers find people difficult and blame them for everything, whether those people are their own bosses or the people in their own teams. In the minds of these negative managers one thing is for sure, it is not them being difficult but everyone else. Subconsciously they project their own problems onto others.

**Negative managers find everything too difficult.**

One modern department store I know adjoins a multi-storey car park. Customers can exit on the fourth floor of the store to access the car park and pay for their parking. At the counter nearest the exit is a large sign stating 'No change given for the car park.' So negative! Yet the company's mission statement includes the phrase, 'We pride ourselves on great service and helping customers.' Why not be delighted to give change for a car park? Why not say 'yes'?

**Choose to be positive in everything you do.**

Choose to be positive in everything you do. Say 'yes' as often possible. Do the things others do not want to do.

Cecilia Estrop, a customer service agent working at Changi Airport in Singapore, frequently has to deal with angry customers. 'I never say "no",' she says, 'this just makes matters worse. I always try to find the best solution to help them.'

'No!' is absolute. It alienates. Regrettably, many managers are experts in saying 'no'. Actually they revel in it. Nothing gives them more pleasure than saying 'no'. The word 'no' reinforces their power over others. 'The buck stops here – and the "stop" word is "no".'

## The negative instrument of the mind

The mind is a negative instrument that has a propensity for the 'no' word while the heart is a positive instrument that loves to say 'yes'. It is the heart that infuses us with such positive qualities as passion and delight while it is the mind that constrains us by pointing out all the risks (essentially negative) of doing this or that.

Cynics will say, 'This is alright in theory but in practice you cannot say "yes" to everyone. Otherwise every employee would be asking for a pay rise, every manager would be asking for an increase in budget and every customer would be asking for substantially discounted price. You have to say "no" when this happens.' The answer to the cynics is simple. If granting the request will generate a positive result *for all concerned* then take the risk and say 'yes'.

Such cynics think only in terms of money. For them the less you give the more profit you make. So they give as little as possible: to employees, to managers and to customers.

## Progressive managers

The progressive managers choose not to think this way. They think in terms of taking risks to seize opportunities to yield positive results. On the occasions when the results are not positive they find a better way. The best company I ever worked for (Mars Ltd) paid their associates (employees) the best wages in the marketplace and had the best value products in the marketplace. You cannot beat a Mars Bar for low price, quality and the overall experience of enjoying a superb chocolate product.

I walked into a small upmarket clothing boutique recently and saw a shirt I liked. It was high quality and expensive. They tried to sell me a second shirt. I liked the second shirt too. So I asked for a discount if I bought two shirts instead of the one intended. Their answer was a blunt 'no'; they couldn't give me a discount. So I walked out without buying either shirt. Even with $1 discount I would have bought the two shirts. I had been the only customer in the boutique. I never see that store busy. I can buy high-quality shirts anywhere.

Nearby was a major department store. I wanted to buy three bottles of perfume for my wife and two daughters. I found a perfume I liked and discovered there was a special offer going with it. If I bought this bottle of perfume I would be entitled to a free toiletry bag filled with high-class goodies. The store assistant brought me the three bottles of perfume but only one free toiletry bag. 'Where are the other two toiletry bags?' I asked. 'This offer is limited to one per customer,' came the reply. So I walked out without buying anything. Revenue down the drain, logic out of the window, fixation with the rules and a propensity to go for the negative choice polarity.

## 'No' as a last resort

I never say 'no' to clients. If they ask for a 10 per cent discount I give it to them because it makes them feel good that they have negotiated me down. I like to make my clients feel good and I love to choose the 'give–take' polarity for this. Yesterday one of my major retail clients asked for 15 *complimentary* copies of my last book. Just one store in this retail chain can take in millions of revenue in a week. In other words, this retail client is in a far better position to pay for these books than I am. Even so I gave them the 15 free copies they requested. I would not dream of going into one of their stores and asking for 15 free shirts or 15 free bottles of perfume. Saying 'no' creates such bad feelings. Saying 'yes' has such a positive effect.

**The more you choose to say 'yes', the more likely people will say 'yes' to you.**

The more you choose to say 'yes', the more likely people will say 'yes' to you. It is what I have described previously as the law of reciprocation: whatever you give out you get back in some shape or form later.

So only choose to say 'no' as a last resort – and that is when you feel you are being badly exploited by another person. But before you get to that point always give the other person the benefit of the doubt and choose to say 'yes'.

**Choosing to say 'yes' is the ultimate choice polarity.**

# CHAPTER SEVEN

# Microbehaviours

## Everything we accomplish in life originates from our choice of microbehaviours

### The nature of behaviour

We tend to talk loosely about behaviour. My Oxford dictionary defines behaviour as, 'the way in which an animal or person responds to a situation or stimulus'. Behaviour relates to conduct and the activities we undertake throughout our lives. It is what we do and how we do it. Good behaviour is helping a blind person cross the road while bad behaviour is ignoring someone who solicits your attention. Good behaviour is writing 'thank you' letters while bad behaviour is swearing at people who upset you.

We all know this. Behaviour is obvious, it is what we see others do and what we do ourselves. As explained in the previous chapters much of our behaviour is automatic, being driven by our subconscious while a minority of our behaviours are well chosen following conscious deliberation.

**Other people can tell us how to behave but in the end it is our choice.**

Behaviour is personal. It belongs to us. It is what we do in response to internal and external stimuli. Other people can tell us how to behave but in the end it is our choice.

### The impact of behaviour on performance

It is behaviour which leads to high or low performance and thus success or failure. Because of the personal nature of behaviour most managers neglect it, preferring to focus on tasks and results in pursuit of their business objectives. Tasks are impersonal. Anybody can do them providing they have been trained. Even robots can undertake tasks. So can computers and dishwashing machines. You set the task, the program runs and the task is completed. That is the task and that is what most managers attempt to concentrate on.

When it comes to people it is slightly different. Behaviour intervenes. The differential between high and low performance, between winning and losing, between success and failure is much more than setting the task and running the programme. The differential relates to people's behaviour on the task.

## Macrobehaviours and microbehaviours

This behaviour can be split into two levels. The first is 'macrobehaviours' which describe high-level behaviours and the second is 'microbehaviours' describing low-level behaviours.

The central thesis in this book is that the major determinant of success in life and work is our choice of microbehaviours. Microbehaviours are all the contributing components to any one macrobehaviour. Microbehaviours are the subsidiary activities that comprise a major activity. They are what goes into doing anything. Microbehaviours are the nuances and minutiae of our *observed* behaviours.

While there is a clear danger that we fail to choose effective macrobehaviours there is an even bigger danger that we totally neglect microbehaviours. However, macrobehaviours are a product of microbehaviours, so the latter cannot be ignored. This is illustrated in Figure 7.1.

**The central thesis in this book is that the major determinant of success in life and work is our choice of microbehaviours.**

The fact that you are reading this paragraph at the moment is an outcome of a whole series of microbehaviours leading to macrobehaviours. You might care to trace how you arrived at this point and the behaviours that led to it.

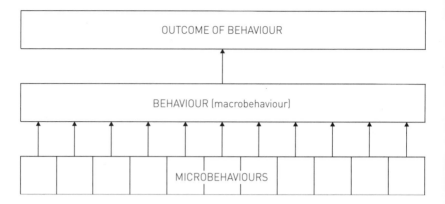

**Figure 7.1**  Macrobehaviours as products of microbehaviours

# Behaviour and outcome

The macrobehaviour is picking up this book and reading it. The microbehaviour is the choice of paragraph you read and how you read it, for example whether you scan it quickly, take in the meaning, not take it in, underline certain sentences, annotate a margin, copy it, memorize it, learn from it, choose to interpret the paragraph in a certain way, read on to the next page, hop to another part of the book or simply put it down and sip some coffee. The outcome is the experience that is created as a result of this behaviour (picking up the book and reading it) and the subsidiary microbehaviours. This outcome could be nothing, a stimulus for further thinking, a valuable lesson or a topic of conversation with another person. It is your choice. You choose the microbehaviours, the macrobehaviours and the outcomes. The interrelationship between the three is 'iterative'. Before we choose our microbehaviours we have to choose the desired outcome and the macrobehaviour. During the cyclical process that takes place our microbehaviours can be amended if we sense the desired outcome is not being accomplished. This cyclical process is indicated in Figure 7.2.

The key point to stress here is that our choice of microbehaviours is critical in determining the outcomes of our chosen macrobehaviours. Should we

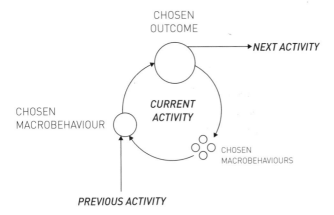

**Figure 7.2**   The cyclical process of behaviour

choose a different set of microbehaviours then the nature of the chosen macrobehaviour will change and the outcome will be different.

## Non-accomplishment of outcomes

It should also be pointed out that the chosen outcome is not always accomplished. This might be for four reasons:

1   We choose inappropriate outcomes (e.g. when we choose expectations that are too high: for example expecting someone always to agree with us)

2   We choose inappropriate microbehaviours (e.g. we sound too formal when an informal approach would be more effective)

3   We choose inappropriate macrobehaviours (e.g. we instruct rather than consult)

4   External events (outside our control) occur (e.g. the other person is in a bad mood)

It is worth giving some further examples of microbehaviours in relation to a chosen macrobehaviour (Box 7.1).

| BOX 7.1 | Choice of macrobehaviour |
| --- | --- |

| **Example 1:** | **Example 2:** |
| --- | --- |
| **Making a phone call** | **Walking through an office** |

CHOICE OF MACROBEHAVIOUR

| | |
| --- | --- |
| Stand up while calling | Speed of walking |
| Sit down while calling | Route through office |
| Attitude | Demeanour |
| Tone of voice | How many people to initiate contact with |
| | How to initiate contact |
| | How to respond to others who initiate greeting |
| Style of greeting | Style of greetings |
| Feelings about person being called | Feelings about person in contact with |
| Emotions 'tagged' to microbehaviours | Emotions 'tagged' to microbehaviours |
| Length of call | Length of interaction with any one person |
| % Informal chit-chat | % Informal chit-chat |
| % Formal discussion | % Formal discussion |
| % Talking | % Talking |
| % Listening | % Listening |
| Humour used | Humour used |
| Topics covered | Topics covered |
| Questions asked | Questions asked |
| Degree of interest taken | Degree of interest taken |
| Fiddle/doodle while talking | Body language while talking |
| Responses promised | Responses promised |
| Follow up intentions | Follow up intentions |
| Whether or not to take notes | Whether or not to take notes |
| How to conclude call | How to conclude interaction |
| *etc.* | *etc.* |

To make choices about microbehaviours requires a considerable amount of energy. It is hard work and that is why many people neglect them. When this happens microbehaviours are generated automatically, without thinking. We become unaware of the frown on our face and the harsh tone of our voice. We become unable to see ourselves for what we are because we have lost sight of all the little behaviours (microbehaviours) that comprise our demeanour, our gait, our communication and the general way we conduct ourselves through our daily working lives.

> **To make choices about microbehaviours requires a considerable amount of energy.**

A lack of focus on microbehaviours can thus lead to undesirable consequences by which we inadvertently upset people because they have misread our motives. They have picked up signals from our microbehaviours which have been misinterpreted or which are in conflict with what we have been saying and doing.

## Microbehaviours and reading small signals

All species of animal, including human beings, excel at reading small signals. It is how we survive. A dog will carefully watch his master's eyes and listen carefully to his tone of voice to gauge the signals. The dog will respond as appropriate, wagging its tail or shivering with fear according to these microbehaviours.

The same will apply in any human situation. We can tell whether or not a person is confident from his or her microbehaviours, we can tell whether or not they are serious or having us on. We make these judgements all the time. It is easy to say that we should take people at face value but, in fact, most of us rarely do this. Invariably, we use our nous to determine what is really going on inside another person's head and heart. That nous is our innate intelligence for reading and interpreting other people's microbehaviours. We see the look in their eyes (a microbehaviour) and know instantly what is going on. We take a call and know instantly from the tone of voice (a microbehaviour) that there is a problem.

> **We use our nous (our innate intelligence) to determine what is really going on inside another person's head and heart.**

# Character patterns and microbehaviours

These microbehaviours add up to establish a pattern that characterizes the type of person we are. People judge us on this, they form opinions on our pattern of microbehaviours. Our character is not just based on macrobehaviours (deciding to telephone someone) but on our microbehaviours (how we apply energy to the microbehaviours which formulate the call).

The outcomes which we experience in life and at work are thus determined to a high degree by these microbehaviours. It is not through the activities we take (like working hard and studying intensively) but through the microbehaviours we put into these activities.

As stressed in a previous chapter there is no guarantee that any one set of microbehaviours will generate the outcomes or successes we desire in life. Randomness and luck have a huge part to play. However, we can increase the probability of our success by focusing on our microbehaviours, which are often neglected, to determine those which are positive and most effective. We can also increase the range of microbehaviours we adopt, for example, using different words for improved effect or trying different ways such as a more cheerful tone of voice. Gradually, these changes will add up to something significant. The process is evolutionary. We do not see a person ageing, we do not see the grey hairs growing, we do not see the widening of the waistline – but we do know that after a year or so that person is that much older, greyer and fatter. In other words, if you weigh yourself before and after eating a chocolate bar you will detect no difference in weight. However, if you eat 1,000 chocolate bars in a year you will see and measure a difference.

**All our microbehaviours evolve into a pattern which influences our future direction.**

Indulging in a chocolate bar is a microbehaviour and forms one of many that goes into the overall macrobehaviour of eating. The pattern of eating leads to the type of person we are and by which other people perceive us. The same applies to every little thing we do at work. Our tone of voice, our demeanour, our attitude, our choice of words all evolve into a pattern that influences our future direction.

## Choosing more effective microbehaviours

Thus to improve we have to examine the pattern and choose microbehaviours that are more likely to achieve the outcome we desire: being a more effective person.

In the multitude of self-help books available in this day and age too much attention is given to macrobehaviours and prescriptions for these. For example, many of the books I have studied recently focus on the importance of such steps as (i) establishing a purpose or vision, (ii) becoming self-disciplined, (iii) sustaining focus, (iv) controlling one's destiny, (v) developing great teams and (vi) learning from adversity. The self-help book I have open in front of me lays out 17 principles of success.

**In most self-help books and training courses there is a lack of attention to choosing effective microbehaviours.**

However, each is defined in terms of macrobehaviours. They are behaviours such as 'communicate effectively' and 'inspire your team'.

Every single manager in the world knows that he or she must 'communicate effectively' and 'inspire his or her team'. It sounds so easy; it is amazing that so few managers practise this. The reason relates to a lack of attention to choosing effective microbehaviours. It is the build-up of microbehaviours that determines whether communications are effective or not or whether teams are inspired or not. Communication and inspiration are merely the high-level macrobehaviours and thus easy to proclaim, as most textbooks and teaching courses do.

## The infinite range of microbehaviours

The difficulty comes with the millions of miniscule microbehaviours. There can be no specific prescription for these, any more than we can specify in detail what the perfect human being does. The range of microbehaviours available to us is infinite and the intention of this book is NOT to prescribe a perfect set of 17 microbehaviours which will guarantee success for any manager.

To improve our performance we constantly need to challenge our microbehaviours and to determine whether there are more effective ones from which we can choose. In doing so we submit ourselves to an evolutionary process by which ineffective microbehaviours become discarded while building on those that are more effective. The one thing we must do, and perhaps this *is* a prescription, is to become conscious of these microbehaviours and the impact they have in determining the outcomes and experiences we desire. We cannot allow ourselves to lapse into a low-energy approach in which our subconscious drives us all the time. In this way we become brain dead, mediocre and creatures of habit.

**To improve our performance we constantly need to challenge our microbehaviours.**

# PART THREE

# Three essential practices for 'How to choose'

**H**   Hesitation

**O**   Outcomes (choose)

**W**   Way (widen the way using 'W-thinking')


The 'HOW' method of choosing is aimed at enhancing your performance as a manager by increasing the number of opportunities, potential outcomes and macro- and microbehaviours from which to choose.
By increasing these you will increase the probability of success for
your team and yourself.

It is based on three simple 'HOW' practices: The first relates to hesitation (H), the second to choosing outcomes (O)  and the third to
generating the necessary behaviours by widening (W) the way using
'W-thinking' (wobbly thinking) as opposed to linear 'I-thinking'.
'W-thinking' enables us to extend the range of options from which to
choose and thus become more effective.


**Chapter 8**
deals with HESITATION in the context of the thesis presented in the
preceding chapters

**Chapter 9**
deals with choosing OUTCOMES

**Chapter 10**
deals with widening the WAY using 'W-thinking' (wobbly thinking)

# CHAPTER EIGHT

# Practice 1: Hesitation

| | |
|---|---|
| **H** | Hesitation |
| **O** | Outcomes (choose) |
| **W** | Way (widen the way using 'W-thinking) |

## The need for hesitation: Setting the scene

As stressed throughout this book most things we do are driven by our subconscious. Our conscious brain is such a slow cumbersome device that we simply do not have time to think everything through. To do so would consume vast amounts of energy and get us virtually nowhere. For example, we tie up our shoelaces without even thinking HOW to do it. We simply do not have time to think through every move and consciously decide every time that, 'this lace goes over this one and this one under that one'. We just do it without thinking as a result of preset programmes in our subconscious. Our subconscious is loaded to the hilt with such programmes which emanate either from our inherited genes or from subconscious learning from past experiences. In other words, we have to rely on our subconscious to drive most of our behaviour. These subconscious drives become our habits and the daily routines which consume much of our time.

The route along which we drive to the office every morning is invariably the same. We do not even think about it. We drive along it out of habit. We only choose a different route when there is an emotional stimulus to move out of routine (for example, roadworks causing a traffic jam).

**We easily get into 'routine' or 'mechanistic' mode because it is easy, it requires little energy and we do not need to think.**

When we drive into the car park every morning we hardly think where we are going to park, we automatically look for the space nearest the entrance and park there. We do it without thinking. In fact, our minds might be elsewhere, chatting away on the cell phone or contemplating the first meeting of the day.

When we enter the meeting we rarely think about the greeting we are going to use and tend to use the same one each time. We easily get into routine or mechanistic mode because it is easy, it requires little energy and we do not need to think. That is the purpose of having habits: to make life easy for us.

## Issues of substance vs microbehaviours

As managers we often delude ourselves that we conserve our thinking energies for the more important issues of substance, for example, what we are going to say in front of our director or what we are going to write to a customer. We like to think that our thinking energies should be devoted to important matters such as devising plans or making crucial decisions on how to allocate resources.

However, important decisions are, by definition, rarely made. It is not as if every minute of the day we, as managers, are choosing whether or not to allocate a $1,000 or $10,000 resource to A, B or C. Such decisions do occur but are infrequent in comparison with all the other things we do on a daily basis but which we give little thought to, such little things as choosing to grab a coffee, open the e-mail, talk to a secretary, read the newspaper, glance out of the window, make eye contact with a team member, say thank you, tap our feet, scratch our head, frown or even smile. Most times we are not even conscious of these little things we do. Yet it is these little things we do (our microbehaviours) that have a major impact on people – not just the big things or important matters that we like to think we are here for as managers.

**It is the little things we do that have a major impact on people.**

Just listen to your colleagues talking about other people. Invariably, it is the little things they comment upon. For example, 'I didn't like the way she looked at me when I suggested I come in late tomorrow' or 'I find it so irritating the way he taps his pen and looks out of the window when I am talking to him.'

## The microbehaviours of senior executives

The importance of microbehaviours also applies to the most senior people in an organization, for example, CEOs. They might like to delude themselves that their main task is to choose between strategic options which have a major impact on their companies' future fortunes. These options might relate to investing millions on a refurbishment project, a culture change initiative, a new product development programme, a major sales push or a financial retrenchment. They might also include making an important organizational change or establishing a new team at the top. But CEOs will delude themselves if they believe that it is only the choice of strategic options which has a major impact on the business. Equally important, if not more so, are the multitude of small things or microbehaviours about which most CEOs rarely think. It is these little things that CEOs do that ripple through an organization and create waves of either discontent or support. Who the CEO chats to en route through the office will have an important influence on the future of the company as well as what he says and whether or not he listens to people. His mood will be judged and his emotions examined by all those within his vicinity and these impressions will have a tremendous impact on the day-to-day affairs of the business. Should these impressions be negative they will eventually wear away the fabric of the organization and the business will suffer as a result.

| A KEY PRINCIPLE FOR 'How to choose' is therefore |
| --- |
| Every single thing you do as a manager, no matter how small or big, has an impact on your own performance and that of the team |

# Practice 1:   'H' – 'Hesitation'

The essential step in applying this principle is 'hesitation' in advance of every microbehaviour. This requires immense energy and is incredibly hard work. The 'hesitation' might just be for a second or five seconds but should not be for too long (in which case it would not be hesitation but procrastination).

Through hesitation we allow ourselves momentarily to stall any impending microbehaviour and reconsider its emotional (feel good or feel bad) impact on other people and thus the business. It enables us to reflect on the outcomes of such a behaviour and decide whether or not such an immediate outcome leads to the desired outcomes and performance we desire in the longer term. In the absence of hesitation we allow our behaviours to be driven by our subconscious. Hesitation enables the necessary deliberation for choosing considered behaviours and outcomes.

Expressions of irritation, anger, annoyance, exasperation and frustration are examples of microbehaviours which are frequently not moderated by our hesitating conscious mind. Often we do not even realize we look displeased. Our subconscious is pulling muscles in our face to display negativity without our even knowing it.

Our subconscious works behind our back and frequently tries to outmanoeuvre our scheming conscious mind. We pretend to be happy when everyone knows we look unhappy. We act out a role of welcome when our body language indicates that we do not welcome this person at all. Hypocrisy is the battle between the true feelings which are often hidden away in our subconscious and the artificial feelings we try to put on show for others in the interests of diplomacy. Sometimes we are not brave enough to be open and speak our minds. When this happens our chosen words frequently come into conflict with our instinctive gestures and facial expressions. That is why so many people are deemed to be false. Their conscious attempts to control behaviour are inconsistent with the countermovements of their subconscious

**Our subconscious works behind our back and frequently tries to outmanoeuvre our scheming conscious mind.**

drives. Because they are not being true to their own selves they come across to others as being untrustworthy and unreliable. Their eyes go in the opposite direction of their words. They say one thing and do another. They do not practise what they preach. They pay lip service to a cause they do not espouse. All the time it is the battle between the subconscious where the true self is hidden and the conscious which aims to act out a self of which others will accept and approve. However, even the subconscious is not perfect and it frequently drives us into behaviours which do not reflect our true self. When this happens the conscious mind, through hesitation, can intervene and correct our imperfect impulse with the choice of a better behaviour. This is the benefit of a momentary hesitation.

## The benefits of hesitation

Hesitation is thus absolutely necessary for us to reflect on each impending microbehaviour and reconcile it with our true self, as well as reflect upon the potential outcome of such an impending behaviour whether it be a scowl, an angry word or ignoring a person you do not like. Hesitation enables us to use our conscious mind to get in touch with our heart and soul, flush away negative emotions and replace them with positive ones. Hesitation provides us with an opportunity to stop the scowl, prevent the cutting remark, avoid the look of despair and replace them with positive gestures which genuinely reflect the positive energy we have chosen to generate in our hearts and souls.

The old saying 'fools rush in where others fear to tread' is pertinent here. As managers we should never rush in. We should always hesitate, always consider the impact of our behaviour on others and the dramatic effect it might have on team morale and organizational climate. This does not mean we should not be naturally spontaneous (if that is our 'true self'). Even spontaneity can be enhanced by half a second's hesitation. There are always choices on how we express our natural self, for example, on how much energy we put into a smile, on the way we smile and whether or not we should smile in the first place. Often others are suspicious of those with a permanent smile on their face. A smile should be our

**Even spontaneity can be enhanced by half a second's hesitation.**

conscious choice. As soon as we allow a smile to be produced automatically by our subconscious the danger is that the smile paradoxically becomes false. By having a smile on frequent display we fail to differentiate between external stimuli which would justify a smiling response and those which do not. A permanent smile cannot differentiate between those stimuli which justify a smile and those which do not. A permanent smile can thus never be genuine. At this moment I am completely alone typing away in my study. I am not smiling. Why should I smile at the screen? We should only smile when other people give us something to smile about or when we want to give other people something to smile about. All other smiles are false.

So hesitate very briefly before you smile and consider why you are smiling. Then, if you choose to smile, choose to convey it with all your heart and all the warm emotional energy that you have available. Like all choices, choosing to smile is a conscious emotional choice.

## Emotional conversion

The same practice of hesitation should apply to virtually everything we do. It means raising from the subconscious to the conscious all the impending behaviours that potentially have an impact on other people and reconsidering them in the light of their potential outcome. Many of these are the microbehaviours of which we are normally unaware. Hesitation is the practice of energizing our conscious mind to intervene between our subconscious drives and the overt behaviours they automatically produce. If the drives and behaviours are legitimate, in terms of our own personal values and beliefs as well as in terms of the positive impact they might have, then our conscious mind should allow them to proceed. Such hesitation should only take a fraction of a second. However, if, on consideration, we find that our impending behaviour is negative or conflicts with our personal values and beliefs or will make another person feel bad then we should convert it into a positive behaviour. We should convert an instinctive frown into a genuine smile. For example, should we experience rage and the instinctive urge to thump someone (or if you are a manager to shout at a subordinate) then we should hesitate and

**Hesitation means raising from the subconscious to the conscious all our impending behaviours and reconsidering them.**

in doing so attempt to convert the impending negative behaviour into something more positive (for example, a kind word of advice). This is the process of emotional conversion (Box 8.1).

| BOX 8.1 | Practice 1 – Hesitate |

**Hesitate** before you act
**Hesitate** before you react
**Hesitate** before you choose
**Hesitate** before you communicate
**Hesitate** (H) in order to consider the outcomes (O) and the WAY (W) you are going to accomplish them. This is the essential practice in HOW to choose

### Examples
When with another person or in the vicinity of other people you will need to apply the practice of momentary **Hesitate**.

For example, **Hesitate** before **Choosing** ...

... facial expressions *(e.g. whether to show delight or disinterest)*
... the look in your eyes *(e.g. to make eye contact or to look away)*
... your gestures *(e.g. to cross your arms or to wave your hands around)*
... the words you use *(e.g. the same greeting as last time or something different this time)*
... your immediate direction *(e.g. which way to walk through the office, who to talk to)*
... every single action *(e.g. whether or not to shut the door or leave it open)*
... every single reaction *(e.g. what to say – if anything - when someone provokes you)*

Whatever your choice, rest assured it will have an impact one way or another on others and that an accumulation of repeated (same) choices over a period of time will create a pattern of behaviour by which others judge you and which will thus have an impact on their own behaviour and performance.

**Whatever your choice, rest assured it will have an impact.**

## Hesitation is not procrastination

It should be stressed that the practice of hesitation is not the same as procrastination. Hesitation is no more than a momentary (a few split seconds') delay in making a choice while procrastination is a deliberate attempt to put off making a decision for a long period of time. Hesitation is a brief consideration or short deliberation of the consequences of what you are about to do with the purpose of identifying more effective behaviours and outcomes. Hesitation relates to the immediate. It relates to a momentary pause in choosing a response to an external stimulus (such as someone entering our office).

It should further be stressed that hesitation is hard work. It requires energy to create the consciousness necessary to consider (and reconsider) all those behaviours and microbehaviours that have an impact on performance. As previously stated most people rely on the low energy ease of subconscious routine to drive their daily work habits. This leads to impulsive or automatic behaviour. It is all too easy to do things without thinking. Hesitation overrides these subconscious drives by applying second thoughts to each impending behaviour and its potential outcome.

# CHAPTER NINE

# Practice 2: Choosing outcomes

**H** Hesitation

**O** Outcomes (choose)

**W** Way (widen the way using 'W-thinking)

The second essential practice in the 'HOW to choose' method relates to OUTCOMES (O). Everything we do in life should have a purpose. This means that every single thing we do should be geared to a preconsidered and desired outcome. While others might attempt to impose that purpose on us we should ideally choose our own purpose. Purpose answers the question, 'Why are we doing this?'

**Every single thing we do should be geared to a preconsidered and desired outcome.**

A purpose leads to a desired outcome. When the outcome is not desired the purpose has not been accomplished. Something else has happened that we did not want. Expressed another way an outcome is the totality of experiences that result from a cluster of intended (purposeful) behaviours together with unintended (non-purposeful) behaviours.

## Differentiating between outcomes and objectives

An outcome is different from an objective, the latter being measurable (for example in terms of time and money) while an outcome is rarely measurable. This is illustrated in Figure 9.1.

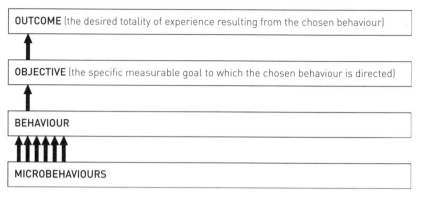

**Figure 9.1**  Outcome and objective

While an objective can be specific and measurable, an outcome is emotional and relates to how people feel. For example, the pictures of people sunning themselves on paradise beaches are portrayals of the outcomes travel agents seek to promote in their brochures. 'We offer you paradise' is the outcome travel agents subtly and indirectly promote, even though they can never commit to this. They can never guarantee an outcome in which the vacation is thoroughly enjoyable and lives up to the fantasy image created in the customer's mind. All the travel agent can do is guarantee the objective of flying the customer to a specific destination and providing specified accommodation together with specific facilities. The objective is specific and measurable. There will be an aeroplane, the flight will take six hours, there will be transportation from the airport to the hotel, the accommodation will include a spacious room and a buffet breakfast will be provided. That objective can be guaranteed as part of the contract. It is measurable. An outcome cannot be guaranteed and is rarely measurable. No one can guarantee the weather or that things will not go wrong. No one can guarantee the outcome of an 'enjoyable' vacation.

**An 'outcome' cannot be guaranteed and is rarely measurable.**

As a manager you might agree with your team an objective that your area will become the number one performer in the country within 12 months. This objective can be measured in many ways, some financial, others non-financial. However pursuit and accomplishment of the objective must be differentiated from the potential outcomes. These can be either negative or positive. For example, staff might become demotivated as a result of the stress they feel they are suffering from 'having bitten off more than they can chew'. Alternatively, they might become highly motivated by the praise and adulation that is increasingly heaped on them as progress is made. These are examples of outcomes.

## The outcome of success

It is therefore important to differentiate between an 'objective' and an 'outcome'. While outcomes can never be guaranteed, it is indeed outcomes that determine our future success. In fact, 'success' is an outcome. The outcome of success includes the outcome of 'high reputation' and the 'feeling among many that this team is great'. Outcomes are thus emotional and relate to feelings and perceptions.

Your objective might be to hire some new talent while the outcome might be that the new talent totally disrupts the spirit in the current team by challenging existing ways and outshining existing performers.

**Outcomes are emotional and relate to feelings and perceptions.**

# The limitations of 'management by objectives'

Traditional 'management by objectives' is thus limited to achieving objectives while ignoring the all-important outcomes that have a vital impact on the future of any business. Similarly, the recent trend towards establishing visions and mission statements also has the tendency to neglect outcomes. Too many company boards establish mission statements which are no more than sets of words which comprise neither measurable objectives nor feel good outcomes.

High performance is not only achieving measurable objectives which stretch an individual or a team but also accomplishing successful outcomes which make people feel good. The two are frequently different.

Managers, therefore, need to start by choosing outcomes which will make them and their teams feel good in the short, middle and long term. As soon as the outcomes have been broadly defined it will then be possible to develop specific objectives which maximize the probability of these 'outcomes' being accomplished.

> **A KEY PRINCIPLE FOR** 'How to choose' is therefore
>
> In setting specific objectives it is essential that managers and their teams also choose a set of desirable outcomes that will make them and everyone involved with them (colleagues, customers, suppliers, managers, senior executives etc.) feel good

## Potential conflicts between outcomes and objectives

Trying to set objectives in the absence of any understanding of desired outcomes is very dangerous. It forces people down a task driven route leading to a destination they do not desire. The proliferation of bureaucracy in many companies is an example of this. The objective might be to complete the paperwork by the end of the day and to have it 'figure perfect' (that's quality!) while the outcome might be alienation of customers who are neglected by frontline people concentrating on form filling. You will see this everywhere. In the hotel where I am staying at the moment the housekeeping staff have quality standards to achieve (their objectives) and this is monitored closely by supervisors who come and knock at my door when I am having an afternoon nap and have forgotten to display the 'do not disturb' notice. All they want to do is check my room to see that everything is all right. But they define 'all right' by their own hotel standards, not by my own 'customer' standards. The outcome is that I feel irritated in their attempt to attain their standards. Thus one of their housekeeping staff always moves my wastebin back to the place under the table where it should have been according to their standards rather than leave it in the place where I like, just by the side of my chair. Similarly, when they come to 'turn my bed' they invariably draw the curtains when I want them left open. They are acting according to their own standard objectives as opposed to creating positive outcomes for customers.

**Outcomes are vague and are not easily subjected to precise definition.**

Outcomes are normally vague and are not easily subjected to precise definition. They come in broad brush terms such as 'total customer satisfaction', 'highly motivated staff' and 'excellent reputation' which do not lend themselves to quantitative measures. Attempts to apply quantitative measures to outcomes merely convert them into specific objectives and thus divorce them from the essential emotional attributes associated with outcomes. In other words, as soon as you apply a measure to an outcome it ceases to become an outcome but instead is converted to a specific objective. It might sound like a truism but objectives are objective while outcomes are subjective.

**Objectives are objective while outcomes are subjective.**

## Long-term and short-term outcomes

Outcomes are not only long term (such as having a reputation for being the best service provider in the industry) but, more importantly, are also short term. Sharon Salehi, who works in customer relations at the Bradford and Bingley Bank in the UK, states: 'I want every customer who rings me to have a good memory of me when they put the phone down.' The 'good memory' she refers to is a short-term, albeit ongoing, outcome. It can never be measured specifically and thus could never be measured as an objective. Customer satisfaction surveys do not measure good memory for the simple reason that the concept is too nebulous. As indicated above as soon you attempt to measure customer satisfaction you risk losing sight of what it actually is. An outcome is an experience. Customer satisfaction is such an experience, even if it is a feel good experience. As soon as you attempt to measure the percentage occasions customers are greeted and how many times customers rate the service ten out of ten you railroad yourselves

**How do you rate your marriage? How do you rate happiness?**

into a set of dangerously misleading data divorced from the reality of experience as perceived by customers. Data can never define outcomes but only define narrow subsets relating to specific objectives. How do you rate your marriage? How do you rate happiness? Please do not delude yourself that you can apply meaningful and quantifiable measures to the state of your marriage or to happiness. A happy marriage is an outcome. Your objective might be to go out together every Friday evening in order to share your experiences of the week but accomplishing this objective by no means guarantees the outcome of a happy marriage. It helps.

Similary, setting the objective of a weekly half-hour team meeting to ensure that everyone is up to date with what is going on and understands the current situation by no means guarantees the outcome of a motivated team perceived as successful by all around. It helps.

# Choose your outcomes

The second practice in 'HOW to choose' is thus to CHOOSE YOUR OUTCOMES (O) as well as choosing your objectives.

Everything you do has an outcome. You therefore need to consider all the potential outcomes of all your behaviours.

Box 9.1 contains some examples of short-, middle- and long-term outcome choices to illustrate the practice.

| BOX 9.1 | Outcome choices |

*Short term*
What is the outcome of my arriving late on Monday morning? What are my choices relating to this?
What is the outcome of me, as junior, approaching the president's office, walking through his open door and having a brief chat about progress?
What outcome do I desire for a new recruit on the very first morning of that person's joining my team? What are my choices relating to this?

*Middle term*
What is the outcome the team and I desire when the new CEO visits our department next week? What choices do we have between now and then?
What is the outcome we desire when our senior salesperson retires at the end of the month? What choices do we have in relation to this?
What is the outcome we desire when we take the team away for a retreat next month? What choices do we have in relation to this?

*Long term*
What is the outcome we desire when the CEO reports to the board at the end

of the year on our department's contribution? What choices do we have in relation to this?

What will be the outcome, in our customers' eyes, at the end of the year, of all formal initiatives the company has taken to improve service? What choices do we have in relation to these initiatives?

What will be the outcome for us at the end of the year of the major training programme the company started last month? What choices do we have in relation to this?

It should be stressed that outcomes can never be guaranteed no matter how hard you strive to accomplish them. As objectives are more specific and frequently measurable their achievement is more probable. However, outcomes are rarely within the total control of those desiring such outcomes. Thus they can *never* be guaranteed.

**Outcomes are rarely within the total control of those desiring such outcomes.**

## Outcome probabilities

Furthermore, the probability of an outcome being accomplished decreases the longer term it is. Should a customer ring me at this very minute there is a high probability that I can choose microbehaviours that ensure an outcome that the customer has a good memory of me. The probability that 1,000 customers will have good memories of all their interactions with team members over the next year is substantially less, no matter what objectives we set and how intent our endeavours are. Remember that an outcome is the totality of experience (of all involved) that results from a cluster of intended and unintended behaviours directed towards an objective.

# Linking outcomes to behaviours and principles

The practice of choosing desired long-term outcomes requires lengthy consideration while choosing short-term (immediate) outcomes requires hesitation. During this period of hesitation we will need to link each of our intended immediate behaviours to a potential outcome or, conversely, choose a desired outcome and then link a behaviour to it. For example, what outcome do we desire when we walk into a room full of (i) strangers, (ii) colleagues we know well, or (iii) senior executives with whom we have a fleeting acquaintance?

Not only should both our macro- and microbehaviours be linked to desired outcomes but both should be underpinned by carefully chosen principles. In the absence of obvious principles our behaviours will be viewed as unprincipled and we thus risk undesired outcomes (such as being viewed by others as being untrustworthy, uncaring, inconsiderate or unreliable).

**It is critical that each of our chosen outcomes and linked behaviours be backed up with strongly held principles.** It is, therefore, critical that each of our chosen outcomes and linked behaviours be backed up with strongly held principles. These can only be rooted in the heart and soul and are essentially emotional (although they can, of course, be explained by logic). For example, the principles of trust, care, support and appreciation are emotional. We 'feel trusted' by our boss, we 'feel he cares' for us and 'feel good' when he demonstrates his support for us and his appreciation for all our hard work.

While principles can subsequently be explained by logic they are an integral part of our hearts and souls. They are to do with our essential being. It is essential to BE honest, to BE trusted, to BE a caring person. Principles are not simple deductions from a conscious process of intellectual consideration based on logic, but are at the core of our emotional and spiritual essence. They are rooted in our essential being as human beings; they are rooted in our hearts and souls. Our minds merely explain or justify these deep-rooted feelings that 'we must BE honest, truthful and appreciative'.

## The indestructibility of principles

When it comes to principles we thus have NO choice. They are there whether we like it or not. We cannot escape them. They are irreducible and indestructible and as such form the very nature of our human spirit. These principles form the foundation of most religions, faiths and creeds and thus our communal civilization. We cannot go shopping for principles and choose those we like. Nobody can talk us out of BEING honest, truthful and caring, of BEING appreciative and supportive. These principles are pre-assigned to us the moment we are born. We have no choice in WHAT principles SHOULD apply to our lives and at work. The only choice we have is HOW to apply them and this relates to our choices of outcomes and behaviours.

Principles are there for us to discover and apply in our quest to be better citizens of the world. Furthermore, we have a choice in challenging ourselves (and others) in HOW to apply these principles. In the rush of our everyday lives it is easy to lose sight of principles and pursue, with ill-thought through behaviours, outcomes that are at variance with our principles. This is at the heart of most conflicts we experience in life, the conflict between principle and application. This leads to the perception and practice of hypocrisy.

Hypocrisy arises when the brain attempts to justify behaviours that are at variance with our known principles. It arises when the emotional energies needed to support and express the principles rooted in our hearts and souls are overridden by a simple logic to behave in a selfish way. That is why so many bosses do not practise what they preach. They say one thing and do another. It is called lip service. The brain applies the words to the lips. But it is all mouth. The feelings, in conflict with the words, are hidden and not expressed.

> **Hypocrisy arises when the brain attempts to justify behaviours that are at variance with our known principles.**

## The 'push–pull' effect of principle

Ideally, principles should have a 'push–pull' effect on all our choices whereby they 'push' our behaviours towards outcomes which 'pull' these behaviours through (see Figure 9.2).

At this point it is worth summarizing: Objectives have to be differentiated from outcomes. High performance is an objective while success is an outcome. Outcomes can never be guaranteed and also it is very difficult to forecast them. However, by focusing on an outcome there is an increased probability that it will be accomplished.

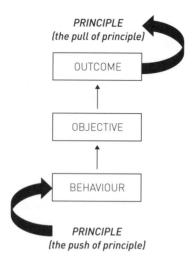

**Figure 9.2**   The push–pull effect of principle

Desired outcomes are essentially emotional and based on perceptions which focus on feel good factors. To that extent they tend to be vague and difficult to define and measure while objectives tend to be specific and relatively easy to define and measure.

Furthermore, our choice of outcomes and behaviours should be underpinned by heartfelt principles.

It is also worth summarizing at this stage the practical steps that can be taken in choosing outcomes and behaviours (Box 9.2).

---

**BOX 9.2**  **Practical steps**

Choose a desired OUTCOME for each intended macro- and microbehaviour
Choose macro- and microbehaviours for each DESIRED OUTCOME
Ensure that each desired OUTCOME and linked behaviour is underpinned by a strongly held principle (or value or belief)

---

*Example*

Consider this, for example, in relation to outcomes, behaviours and principles. When two people get married the objective is to 'tie the knot' at a wedding ceremony as well as arrange a sumptuous celebration for invited guests. The desired outcome beyond the wedding is a 'happy marriage'. The principles underpinning a happy marriage are well known and are based on, for example, mutual fidelity, mutual honesty, mutual caring and mutual support. Marital behaviours are meant to be based on these principles in order to secure the outcome of a happy marriage. The paradox is that in the western world one-third of marriages end in divorce. This is an outcome nobody desires on the day of the wedding. It is an outcome which reflects the behavioural choices we make during our marriage and the way we do, or do not, apply these essential principles.

Thus outcomes (such as success and happiness) while desired and also admirable are very difficult to forecast.

# The application to business

A business is no different. The desired outcome is a happy and successful relationship between employees, managers, shareholders, customers and suppliers. This outcome is emotional and is essential in driving a business forward. If there is NO desired outcome (and desire is emotional) then the probability is that performance will deteriorate. It takes emotional energy (as well as skill and expertise) to achieve high-performance objectives and thus an outcome of success. Success is relative, it is a perception, it is emotional. Other desired outcomes might relate to progress, reputation, esteem, improvement, increased (non-financial) value, personal growth, team spirit, organization 'buzz' and overall satisfaction.

## The need to redefine outcomes

Any manager desirous of improving the performance of his team has therefore to redefine the outcomes with the aim of moving away from the boring low-energy task-driven outcomes (low-level outcomes) to more exciting high-energy challenging and desirable outcomes (high-level outcomes). As soon as these have been broadly defined (it is impossible to define them precisely) then specific objectives can be put in place and the necessary skills, expertise and behaviours developed. The final component in achieving these exciting desirable outcomes is a huge amount of effort, hard work, dedication and commitment. However, this is more likely to be applied by all team members for the simple reason that they will have all subscribed emotionally (from their hearts) to the accomplishment of an outcome which excites them and challenges them. As soon as the outcome is desired (emotionally) then people will have the motivation to strive for it.

**As soon as the outcome is desired (emotionally) then people will have the motivation to strive for it.**

The traditional reliance on merely setting objectives (management by objectives) deprives a manager and his team of the essential emotional component of motivation through agreeing desired outcomes.

Therefore, a set of desired outcomes must be chosen by managers and their teams if there is to be any chance of achieving high-performance objectives.

## Further examples

The following (Boxes 9.3 and 9.4) are two sets of examples of low- and high-performance outcomes from which any manager can choose. The first example relates to senior executives and the longer term outcomes that will arise from their chosen behaviours. The second example relates to managers and the shorter term (daily or weekly) outcomes that will arise from their chosen behaviours.

| BOX 9.3 Example 1: Longer term outcomes | |
| --- | --- |
| Low-performance outcomes | High-performance outcomes |
| *the behaviours of the top team currently lead to the following outcomes ...* | *the behaviours of the top team currently lead to the following outcomes ...* |
| Reactive culture | Proactive culture |
| Status quo (nothing changes) | Boundaries are pushed back (everything changes) |
| Efficient application of the routine | Going beyond the routine to make everyone feel special |
| Sound reputation | Reputation for being progressive |
| Standard approach (whatever the issue) | Dynamic approach (whatever the issue) |
| 'It's okay' (view of customers and staff) | 'It's fantastic' (view of customers and staff) |

| | |
|---|---|
| Little inspiration (for all) | Inspirational (for all) |
| Intelligent organization | An organization with genius |
| Scientifically determined results (reliance on science, research, analysis etc.) | Phenomenally creative using the best tools available |
| Eyes down, people looked bored (general) | Eyes sparkle, people looked excited (general) |
| Low energy environment | High energy environment |
| Few succeed | Everyone succeeds |
| Average grade 'C' – few grade 'A's | Everyone is a winner, everyone is grade 'A' |
| Formal feedback through formal appraisal | Frequent informal feedback on performance |
| Dullness is the norm | Excitement is the norm (a lot of buzz!!!) |
| People are robots | People are human beings |
| People are what their bosses want them to be | People are themselves |
| A high degree of 'sameness' year in year out | Differentiates by being different in every aspect |
| 'This company is not SPECIAL' | 'This company really is SPECIAL' |
| People fear the bosses | People love their bosses |
| Vague satisfaction (customers, staff) | Overall delight with the organization (customers, staff) |
| Lack of motivation (low morale) | High degree of motivation (high morale) |

0    1    2    3    4    5    6    7    8    9    10

**Invite your team to rate your organization (and thus your senior team) on the scale indicated and then discuss the results**

**Then CHOOSE the ideal set of outcomes and develop behaviours to accomplish these (e.g. by way of influencing the senior team)**

| BOX 9.4 | Example 2: Shorter term outcomes |

| Low-performance outcomes | High-performance outcomes |
|---|---|
| *my behaviour as a manager currently leads to the following 'team outcomes'* | *my behaviour as a manager currently leads to the following 'team outcomes'* |
| They often go home at the end of the day tired | They often go home at the end of the day exhilarated |
| They get bored by what they do | What they do excites them |
| They hate going to work | They love going to work |
| They just do the bare minimum | They give everything they have got |
| They do not feel valued | They feel valued |
| They look away when I enter the room | Their eyes light up when I enter the room |
| The atmosphere is flat | There is a high spirit (a buzz!!!) |
| They just go through the motions | They are motivated with their emotions |
| They feel restricted as a result of all the controls | They have total freedom (they can unleash their energies) |
| They do not feel trusted, supported or valued | They feel trusted, supported and valued |
| They have limited experience of success | They experience success daily, monthly and annually |
| They have few challenges (beyond the routine) | They have daily challenges which they love |
| They see problems in a negative light | They approach problems positively |
| There are many who moan, groan and whinge | Everyone is positive |
| There are infrequent celebrations | There are frequent (daily) celebrations |
| There are infrequent diversions (we keep to the routines) | There are frequent diversions (we have fun, games, quizzes, events, etc.) |

0     1     2     3     4     5     6     7     8     9     10

**Invite your team to rate your behaviour as a manager on the scale above and then discuss the results**

**Then CHOOSE the ideal set of outcomes and develop behaviours to accomplish these (e.g. by way of creating a BUZZ!!! within your team)**

Box 9.4, for individual managers, effectively represents 'short-term' outcomes that can be accomplished on a weekly if not daily basis.

The long- and short-term outcomes referred to here are the overall product of choices drawn from a vast range of behaviours available to senior executives and managers. The resulting totality of experience is that people (customers, employees, managers and suppliers) either feel good about the organization and you, their manager, or they feel bad. The desired outcome is that everyone feels good.

Low-performance outcomes occur when managers do NOT focus on desired outcomes, when they are driven by tasks and focus on specific measurable objectives. In doing so they ignore and thus neglect the essential emotional factors that lead to the high performance outcomes. These emotional factors must be factored into all management behaviours and geared to consciously chosen emotional outcomes. When this happens there is an increased probability of high performance (assuming the skills and expertise have been developed and the resources are available).

> **Emotional factors must be factored into all management behaviours and geared to consciously chosen emotional outcomes.**

The HOW to CHOOSE technique therefore requires that a manager carefully chooses the outcomes (O) for his everyday macro- and micro-behaviours as well as for the middle and longer term. These choices must emanate from his heart and soul and be based on principle. In no way can they be solely determined through a rational thought process.

# CHAPTER TEN

# Practice 3: Widen the way (using 'W-thinking')

**H** Hesitation

**O** Outcomes (choose)

**W** Way (widen the way using 'W-thinking)

## 'I-thinking'

The third and final practice of the HOW to CHOOSE methodology is to 'widen the way' in which we choose to behave in seeking a chosen outcome. This enables us to generate a much larger number of macro- and microbehavioural options from which to choose. 'Widening the way' is equivalent to 'broadband thinking'.

As stated previously most times our behaviours are automated along preset rational lines in our subconscious. Such are the routines and habits which dominate our lives.

These automated lines of thinking effectively narrow the way and lead to what I describe as 'I-thinking' or 'narrow-band thinking'.

Basically I-thinking is straightforward. It moves us straight from one step to the next using tried and trusted lines that are entrenched in our minds. I-thinking is doing what we have always done before, probably because it worked for us before (although as time progresses we rarely check out whether it is working for us now). I-thinking is **'I-thinking' is boring.** boring. It does not deviate from previous lines of thinking and is mostly repetitive. It is the same old greeting, the same old handshake, the same old welcome, the same old present at each birthday celebration, the same old routine as last week and the week before and in all probability as the last ten years.

I-thinking is the way most of us think. It tends to be uncontentious because it has been done before. It is merely repeats thinking programmes adopted in our past and is therefore very easy. I-thinking leads to the safety of comfort zones and to self-righteous attitudes. It leads to convention, tradition and conformity. It does not excite but at least it is perceived as both predictable and reliable. When I-thinking occurs we know what to expect, both from ourselves and from others we know well.

**'I-thinking' is the way most of us think.**

I-thinking leads to habits and customs which become accepted as the social norm within various groups. I-thinking is used in training because it programmes people's minds to think in certain ways to adopt the necessary behaviours for tasks to be completed. I-thinking leads to scripted welcomes and the procedures we must use when an untoward situation arises.

I-thinking follows lines of thinking laid down years ago, sometimes by ourselves and sometimes by others. I-thinking is not new; it is old. I-thinking is coercive; it tells us what the next step should be without having to spend too much energy thinking through what that step should be.

I-thinking is arrogant and complacent. It assumes that what we thought before and will again think now is the best way. I-thinking does not challenge anything, it merely instructs you to do what you did before, for example to frown at someone who interrupts you – because you have always frowned at people who interrupt you. I-thinking does not offer us other options. I-thinking does not permit us to review the efficacy of what we do.

I-thinking works in simple straight lines. It is straightforward and works discreetly with our subconscious to dominate our lives. We are hardly conscious of it because it keeps a low profile. We scarcely give a thought to most things we do at work and home. I-thinking is the next thing to the unthinking subconscious mode that drives most of our behaviour.

I-thinking is selfish. It does what 'I' want because that is what 'I' had before and that made me feel good. I-thinking focuses on 'me' (or 'I' as a person).

A cluster of I-words to stimulate your thinking can be found in Box 10.1.

| BOX 10.1 | A cluster of I-words | | |
|---|---|---|---|

**I (=me)**

| | | | |
|---|---|---|---|
| In | Icy | Ill | Impair |
| Innate | Inert | Idle | Inferior |
| Inside | Introvert | Idiocy | Impede |
| Inner | Inhibited | Infirm | Indulge |
| Insular | Impossible | Imperious | Indifference |
| Interior | Impersonal | Ignorance | Indefensible |
| Internal | Immovable | Implausible | Identical |
| Indoors | Inhospitable | Imperfection | Illusive |
| Inward-looking | Improbable | Impenetrable | Id |
| | | | etc. |

### I-thinking

The cluster reveals the downside pattern of I-thinking. There is a high probability that excessive reliance on I-thinking will lead to one or more of the attributes or outcomes indicated in the cluster.

# The pros and cons of 'I-thinking'

However, it would be unfair to be too extreme about I-thinking. Its potentially negative consequences have to be balanced by the positive benefits an automated linear process of thinking generates. Some aspects of I-thinking are essential to our lives. For example, it is vital that we fasten our safety belts and look in the mirror before we drive away in our cars. That is I-thinking at its best. It will tell us to stop at a red light. We will hardly give it a thought but even so this thought (an I-thought) is absolutely necessary.

**Some aspects of 'I-thinking' are essential to our lives.**

It is vitally important that we men check that our trousers are zipped up before leaving the restrooms and, furthermore, that we have previously washed our hands. This requires little thought but even so it is an essential I-thought. There are a million other examples of the benefits that I-thinking can bring.

Conversely, I-thinking can work against us, for example, when our eyes drift away from our guest (or spouse) when an attractive person walks through the door or when we ignore a telephone ringing on someone else's desk.

Together with our subconscious, I-thinking drives most of our minute everyday behaviours and thus has a tremendous impact on the outcomes of our lives. I-thinking effectively negates choice. It does not allow us to choose because the choice has already been made for us by previously programm-emed thinking patterns.

**I-thinking effectively negates choice.**

# Broadband 'W-(wobbly) thinking'

While this book does not advocate an elimination of I-thinking it does favour a restoration of the balance towards 'W-thinking' to widen the way and create a broader range of macro- and microbehavioural options.

To maximize effectiveness and increase the probability of achieving a desired outcome we continually have to challenge ourselves with two iterative questions:

1  What will be the outcome of this next behaviour of mine?
2  What other behavioural options are available to me to achieve the desired (chosen) outcome?

We can widen the way for this by using broadband 'W-thinking' (wobbly or wizard thinking) as opposed to linear I-thinking. The latter is a low-energy thinking procedure while the former is a high-energy process requiring emotional, spiritual and intellectual energy. I-thinking is relatively easy while W-thinking is difficult and challenging.

**I-thinking is relatively easy while W-thinking is difficult and challenging.**

W-thinking is wobbly or wizard thinking. It does not follow a simple straight line (as does I-thinking). W-thinking can go in any direction, it wanders around at random on the watch for the best possible option. Figure 10.1 was used in Chapter 5 on randomness and demonstrates the two types

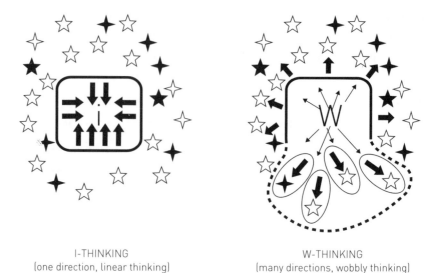

I-THINKING
(one direction, linear thinking)

W-THINKING
(many directions, wobbly thinking)

**Figure 10.1**   I-thinking and W-thinking

of thinking. I-thinking is inward-looking (at me) while W-thinking is outward-looking and can push back the boundaries in any direction.

When we use W-thinking to widen the way we always start in a different position and end in a different position, whereas if we use I-thinking we will always start in the same position and finish in the same position. By doing the latter our competitors will be able to emulate us and overtake us while by doing the former we will always be different from our competitors. Excessive reliance on I-thinking will create vulnerabilities as a result of our predictability whereas balancing it with a healthy dose of W-thinking will create a positive buzz in our relationships which will excite and energize.

## Technique 1:  Word clusters

There are a number of practical techniques that can be used to stimulate W-thinking. One such technique, first used in a previous book[1] of mine, is to use word clusters. Box 10.2 contains an example.

| BOX 10.2 | The upside of W-thinking |
|---|---|

**W (=we)**

| | | |
|---|---|---|
| Wide | Wobble | Weave |
| World | Wizard | Web |
| Win | Wriggle | Willingness |
| Wisdom | Wacky | Warmth |
| Whole | Weird | Wonder |
| Words | Wander | WOW |
| With | Walkabout | Waggish |
| Way | Well | Waves |
| Will | Whizz | Worth |
| WYSIWYG | Watch out | Way out |

| | | | | | |
|---|---|---|---|---|---|
| What? | Why? | Who? | When? | Where? | HoW? |

Some statements using w-words aimed at stimulating your W-thinking in order to widen the way and help you increase the range of behavioural options available to you can be found in Box 10.3.

| BOX 10.3 | Widen the way |
|---|---|

| | |
|---|---|
| **Web** | The bigger your web, the more flies you will trap |
| **Water** | The more bread you sprinkle on water, the greater the probability a fish will bite (but you never know which fish and when) |
| **Walking** | If you keep walking down an endless corridor, sooner or later a door will open |
| **Welcome** | The more people you welcome into your life, the more friends you will have |
| **Wingspan** | The larger your wingspan, the higher you will fly |
| **Wonder** | The more you wonder about life, the more wonderful your life will be (be curious, ask questions, discover things) |
| **Willpower** | The more you will it to happen, the greater the probability it will happen (be determined, keep focus) |
| **Wisdom** | Wise people know they have so much to learn, while foolish people think they know everything |

| | |
|---|---|
| **Watching** | The more people you watch (and listen to), the wiser you become |
| **Wishing** | The one way to make your wishes come true is to help other people make their wishes come true |
| **Wives** | If you stay in your village the whole of your life the probability is that you will marry someone from your village, whereas if you travel the world the probability is that you will marry someone from outside your village |
| **Whole** | To become whole you need to find the holes and fill the holes |
| **Willingness** | The more you say 'yes', the less likely others will say 'no' |
| **Words** | The more words you have, the less you need to use them |
| **Winning** | You only win when you help others win (nobody wants to be a loser) |
| **World** | There is no other world than the one you create for yourself |
| **Warmth** | The heart generates heat while the brain chills you down. Keep warm, be warm but do not be cold or hot-headed |
| **Way** | There is always more than one way ahead |
| **Why?** | W comes before XYZ. Why? (In order to convert the unknown into the known always find the reason first) |

The use of clusters to create patterns is just one way of stimulating your mind to use W-thinking (or wobbly thinking). This first technique is to brainstorm a cluster of words beginning with the same letter and which have a loose generic relationship. Each word must have a different root. The following are additional examples of word clusters drawn from the previously mentioned book:

- best, beauty, brilliant, brightest, biggest, bumper
- cerebral, conscious, clever, conniving, convincing, concise, calculating
- demotivate, deprecate, damage, dreary, dismissive
- excitement, elation, exhilaration, enthusiasm, emotion, energy, electrify
- fear, frown, fight, fright, friction, flinch, flee

For example, we could choose one word from the F-cluster above to create an idea for generating a wider range of options relating to a business situation.

STEP ONE
Choose a word from the F-cluster, e.g. fear

IDEA ⟶ Feeling free to make decisions to 'charge up' the goodwill of our customers

**Figure 10.2** F-cluster idea

Continuing with the F-cluster we can now use the HOW method to widen the range of behavioural options from which to choose in putting into practice this idea (Box 10.4).

| BOX 10.4 | F-cluster: Step 2 |
|---|---|

**H**esitation    To consider carefully the interFACE with each customer we make contact with at the FRONTLINE today

**O**utcome    Enhanced FEELING of goodwill among customers today

**W**ay    **e.g. Apply IDEA to the WAY we greet customers**
*(I-thinking will lead to a routine greeting)*
W-thinking will widen the way by enabling us to choose words and a tone of voice we perhaps do not normally use. For example, we will choose to demonstrate: FRIENDLINESS, FONDNESS, FLAIR or FUN when greeting a customer

**W**ay    **e.g. Apply IDEA to randomly contacting customers to FIND out how they are**
*(I-thinking normally precludes this possibility)*
W-thinking will lead to a choice of opening conversation FORAYS, for example:
- 'I just called to FIND OUT how you were, FREDDIE'
- 'I just wanted to know whether you had FUN on that trip to FLORIDA'
- 'I know you are a FOOTBALL FAN so I decided to ring to FIND OUT what you thought of the match last night'

This cluster technique can be applied using any letter of the alphabet (or any word for that matter). The aim is to use 'W-thinking' to trigger a different way of thinking and to spark new or different ideas. Here is one further example (see Figure 10.3).

**H**

| How? | Heart | Highlight | Helpful |
| Hopeful | Hallmark | Handsome | Happy |
| Harmony | Harvest | Hero | Honourable |
| Highest | Heavenly | Halcyon | Hallelujah! |

STEP ONE
Choose a word from the H-cluster, e.g. heart

IDEA ⟶ Make it 'heavenly' for our customers by putting our heart into helping them

**Figure 10.3**   H-cluster idea

Continuing with the H-cluster use the HOW method to generate a wide range of behavioural options from which to choose in putting into practice the above idea (Box 10.5).

---

**BOX 10.5**   **H-cluster: Step 2**

**Hesitation**   HOW will my next behaviour HELP this lady approaching me?

**O**utcome   This lady feels I have HELPED her and is very HAPPY

**W**ay   **e.g. Apply IDEA to HELPING this lady**
*(I-thinking will lead to a standard response to the lady)*
W-thinking will widen the way with an extended range of behavioural options
- 'I will HELP her through the door'
- 'I will put my HEART in saying HOW pleased I am to see her'
- 'I will HIGHLIGHT the fact that she has completed the form perfectly'

---

- 'I will HOLD her HANDBAG for her while she signs the form'
- 'I will HEED what she has to say to me and answer her HONESTLY'
- 'I will inform her that I will be HAPPY to see her again soon'

# Technique 2: Word of the day

The use of word clusters is just one technique (or mental game) to spark a creative W-thinking thought process to generate further ideas for doing some new or different and thus widening the way.

However, there are many other techniques that can be used for W-thinking. One of my retail clients selects a word of the day to stimulate wobbly thinking about the way today (Box 10.6).

| BOX 10.6 | Word of the day |
|---|---|
| **(example)** | **Widening the WAY – W-thinking – microbehavioural options** |
| Praise | Generate a range of behavioural options to praise people today |
| Smile | Create as many options today to smile at people |
| Special | Go out of your way to make someone feel special today |
| Discovery | Discover something new or different about your customers (or colleagues) today |
| Learn | Learn something new today and review it at the end of the day |
| Greet | Greet twice as many people today as you usually do |
| Passion | Show your passion at least five times today |
| Different | Do something different today |
| Help | Go out of your way to help someone today |
| Chat | Chat to a stranger today and discover something interesting |

# Technique 3: Quote of the day

Another company I know uses a quote of the day to stimulate W-thinking and generate a better way. Here are some examples they use (from my own writings) (Box 10.7).

| BOX 10.7 | Quotes of the day |
|---|---|

- Customer service is a specialism – making each customer feel special
  (*Widen the WAY – W-thinking: What have you done today to make someone feel special?*)
- An effective leader transmits positive energy through an organization
  (*Widen the WAY – W-thinking: In what way did you transmit positive energy today?*)
- The best leaders excite the imagination of their people
  (*Widen the WAY – W-thinking: How have you excited the imagination of your people recently?*)
- Care for your people and they will care for their customers
  (*Widen the WAY – W-thinking: what choices have you made today to care for someone?*)
- People perform best when they like (if not love) what they do
  (*Widen the WAY – W-thinking: Find out what your people love about their work and do more of it*)
- If you like a customer, the probability is the customer will like you
  (*Widen the WAY – W-thinking: What do you like about your customers? How do you show it?*)
- The most important person in the world is the one you are with now
  (*Widen the WAY – W-thinking: How do you show the person next to you that he/she is important?*)

# Technique 4: Extricate yourself

To generate W-thinking and a better way, it is essential that people are extricated from their normal everyday routine environment and exposed to different stimuli. The danger is that if they are confined within the normal daily boundaries they will develop village thinking and become institutionalized.

This can be done through frequent retreats, off-sites, workshops, seminars, training programmes, lunchtime events, travel and trips.

During these 'extrication sessions' teams should have the opportunity of thinking differently, of extricating themselves from their normal mindsets and heartsets by exposure to new and different ways.

# A further example of wobbly W-thinking in choosing to widen the way

Let us imagine you and your friend move into new houses at diagonally opposite ends of a field of new green grass. Your friend invites you over for a drink (see Figure 10.4).

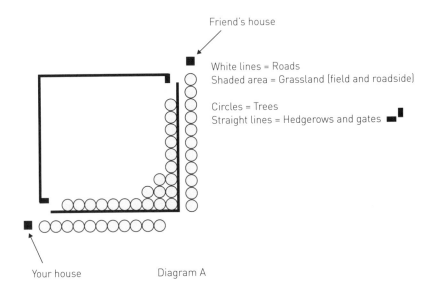

Friend's house

White lines = Roads
Shaded area = Grassland (field and roadside)

Circles = Trees
Straight lines = Hedgerows and gates

Your house                    Diagram A

**Figure 10.4**   W-thinking: What route do you take?

## The I-thinking route

Most people would take the most direct route as indicated in Figure 10.5.

In fact, every time you visit your friend you might use the same direct route. This is I-thinking. Your reasons are simple.

### Reason Set A

1  It is the most direct route

2  It takes the least time and is therefore efficient

3  It is the route you always take and therefore you don't even have to think about it

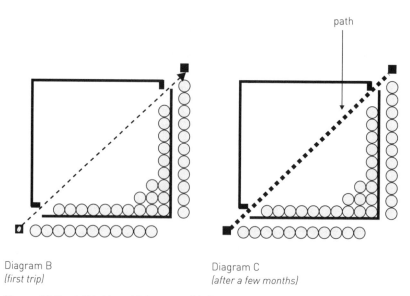

Diagram B
(first trip)

Diagram C
(after a few months)

**Figure 10.5**   I-thinking: Living your life in a straight line

It therefore saves you the energy of having to think about the route. As you leave the field after your first trip you look back. The grass is still green and you cannot see where you have walked. However, over the coming weeks you make the trip regularly and at weekends a few times a day. After a few months you notice the grass has become indented to form a visible path (Diagram C). This is how paths are formed. It is barely noticeable day by day but the growth of grass becomes stunted sufficiently over a period of time to form this path. Each of your microbehaviours (each of your steps) forms this path – but you are unaware of this at the time.

**As you repeat the same activities day in and day out a rut forms in your mind.**

The same thing can happen to your mind. As you repeat the same activities day in and day out a rut forms in your mind. You do not even have to think as you travel along this rut. Such ruts (or paths or tracks) form the routines and habits of everyday life. What is described here is I-thinking. It gives you one option only. When this happens you are living your life in a straight line.

## The W-thinking route

Now consider W-thinking. Every time you visit your friend you choose a different route. The number of routes available to you is infinite. You can walk in any direction you like. You can walk along the roads to the north or east of your house. You can walk round the inside of the field turning left or right as you enter the gate. You can walk round in circles. You can climb over hedges or go through gaps in the hedge. You can study the trees and look for wildlife. You can walk slowly or you can walk quickly. There are innumerable options from which to choose. Two examples are shown in Figure 10.6.

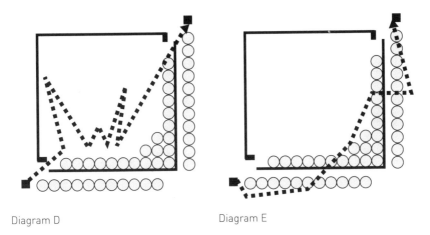

Diagram D                    Diagram E

**Figure 10.6**  W-thinking: Creating and seizing different options

The advantages of W-thinking in this case are as follows.

### Reason Set B

1  The journey takes longer, therefore you have more time to think and meditate

2  The journey takes longer, therefore you have more opportunity to exercise and become fitter

3  The journey takes longer, therefore you have more opportunities to observe what is happening in the field , the hedgerows and the trees

4 The journey takes longer, therefore you will breathe more fresh air

5 You will expose yourself to many more different experiences

6 You will actually think differently

7 You will have many more things to talk about with your friend

8 You will create more variety in your life

9 Your philosophy of life will change (life is more than rushing from point A to point B)

10 You will extricate yourself from the monotony of routine and provide fresh stimuli to your motivation

This simple example can be applied to virtually everything you do in life. In other words, everything you do in life is a CHOICE and potentially a choice between the monotony and comfort of I-thinking and the excitement and creativity of W-thinking. For example, many people come home from work, have a meal and then watch television. That is I-thinking if they do it most nights. Those people who follow the same routine day in and day out are living their lives in a straight line.

W-thinking provides different options. It requires energy but it will energize your life. There are an infinite number of other options from which to choose. Instead of watching television every evening you can use W-thinking to generate the following options (there are so many more) and choose one of them:

1 Read a book

2 Write a book

3 Listen to the radio

4 Go for a long walk

5 Visit the local theatre

6 Learn a new language

7 Undertake some charity work

8 Go swimming at the local pool

9 Write letters to your distant friends

10 Get involved with some community group

11 Listen to a different radio programme every evening

12 Ring up people you haven't spoken to for a long time

You can also compare the differences between I-thinking and W-thinking with most things you do at work.

I-thinking means that you work in a straight line. It means that you:

1 leave for work at the same time every morning

2 take the same route to work every morning

3 park in the same parking place every morning

4 take the same route through the office every morning

5 talk to the same people every morning

6 start your working day off doing the same things every morning

7 have lunch with the same people every day

8 have regular meetings with the same people

9 attend the routine training courses

10 respond to customers in exactly the same way every time

**Your challenge is to apply W-thinking in order to increase the options from which you can choose.**

11 look for the same things in the same reports that you see regularly

12 socialize with the same people at work as you usually do

Your challenge is to apply W-thinking to one or more of these events in order to increase the options from which you can choose. In this way you will develop your worth as a human by exposing yourself to a wider variety of experience.

## Note

1 *What Customers Like About You* by David Freemantle, Nicholas Brealey Publishers, 1998

# PART FOUR

# Applications of 'How to choose'

Part 4 comprises a series of short chapters demonstrating selected applications of 'how to choose'. This selection, while far from exhaustive, picks up on some previous themes and elaborates in terms of practical applications. The selection is presented in alphabetical order and therefore in no particular order of importance. It is suggested the reader 'dip in' to them.

**How to choose:**

CHAPTER ELEVEN

# Choosing assumptions

## To change behaviour we have to choose different assumptions

### Changing your choices to change yourself

The assumptions we make in life directly influence our behaviours and, conversely, the behaviours of others directly influence our assumptions. Thus if we want to change the behaviours of others as well as of ourselves we have to choose different assumptions.

Take punctuality, for example. If we want to change from being an unpunctual person to one who is always punctual we have to change our assumptions about timekeeping before being able to choose microbehaviours that will enable us to be punctual.

Punctual people (and I will choose to coin the word 'punctualists' to describe them) tend to choose a whole set of assumptions that are totally different to those people who are frequently unpunctual.

You might care to discuss with your colleagues whether punctual behaviour has an impact on your long-term successes or otherwise. I would assert that unpunctual people are in all probability likely to be less successful in their lives than punctualists. The choice of punctual microbehaviours produces positive outcomes. Conversely, unpunctual microbehaviours can produce negative outcomes.

Personally, I am never late for meetings. The reason for this is based on the following set of 'choice' assumptions:

- I assume that there is always a probability of a delay en route to the meeting – whether it be a traffic jam, a late train or a delayed flight

- I assume that people will be alienated if I am late for the meeting, and therefore like me less. I don't *want* to be liked less

- I want to be seen as reliable and trustworthy and therefore I assume that if I am always punctual I am more likely to be seen this way

As a result of these assumptions I am generous in the time I allow myself to do anything. I also maintain a constant awareness of the time situation in relation to any self-imposed time deadline. All these contributing factors (generous time allowance, constant awareness of time, self-imposition of time deadlines) are what I describe as microbehaviours.

People who are frequently late make a different set of assumptions which lead to a totally different set of microbehaviours. The types of assumption they make are:

- They assume that a journey that normally takes half an hour will always take half an hour

- They assume that everything will always go to plan

- They assume time will be found for whatever they cram into their schedule

- They assume that people will not be offended if they are late

- They assume that people will understand and accept their reasons for lateness (for example that they were busy, delayed at the previous meeting or held up in the traffic)

People's choice of assumptions are directly linked to their choice of 'yes/no polarities', for example 'yes' this will happen or 'no' this will not happen. It is also linked to their choice of outcomes and chosen foundation of principles, as illustrated in Figure 11.1.

## Assumptions are short-cuts

Assumptions are merely short-cuts that we use in the absence of available information to help us arrive at a behavioural choice.

Many of the world's problems arise because of badly chosen assumptions. For example, when prejudice is rife it is often because of badly chosen assumptions made about certain groups of people. Often we take the wrong

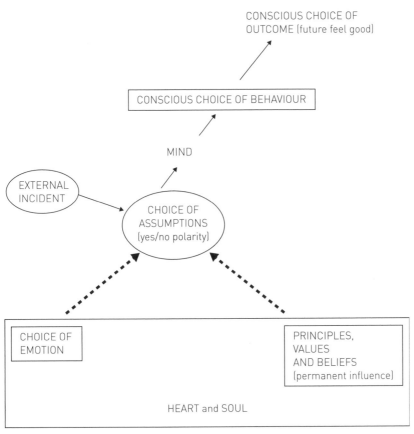

**Figure 11.1** Choice of assumptions and polarities

action (for example, criticizing a person) because we have chosen the wrong assumption about that person's behaviour.

Here are some other examples of badly chosen and correctly chosen assumptions:

| External incident | Badly chosen assumption | Correctly chosen assumption |
|---|---|---|
| **Employee observed making personal call at work** | Employee idling away, chatting to a friend, taking advantage of employer | Employee informing spouse that he/she will be working late this evening |

| Customer with angry look approaches | Customer doesn't like me | Customer thinks it's not my fault |
|---|---|---|
| | Customer is going to make life difficult for me | Customer has problem I can help with |

# Application of the HOW method of choice

By using the HOW method of choice we can re-examine the assumptions we normally make in relation to our chosen outcomes and in this way we can choose new macro- and microbehaviours.

To illustrate this we will revert to the original example relating to punctuality (Box 11.1).

---

**BOX 11.1**  **Application of the HOW method of choice**

**H**esitate    To reconsider the chosen departure time
(and thus re-examine the assumptions we are making about this departure time and the journey time)

**O**utcome    What will be the outcome of arriving early, on time or late? Will it make people feel as good as possible?

**W**ay    W-thinking: Extend the range of macro- and microbehavioural options (in this case relating to journey plans) from which to choose. The final choice might be as follows: Choose to leave one hour early, arrive early and seize the opportunity to (a) drink a coffee and relax (b) go through our papers (c) make a few calls (d) read a book

---

## THE CHOICE CHALLENGE

- Choose your assumptions carefully by creating a conscious awareness of what assumptions you are using in relation to any given behaviour of yours.
- Never make assumptions by imputing to others motives they have yet to reveal (e.g. never assume that this person is against you until such time you have 100% cast-iron evidence that he is).
- Make assumptions based on high probabilities. For example, the probability that there will be a traffic jam delaying you for half an hour is high while the probability that the traffic jam will last for five hours is low.

# CHAPTER TWELVE

# Choosing bosses

## In the 21st century it is people who will be choosing their bosses

### Historical perspective

Throughout history it has always been assumed that employers have the power and that employees should bow and scrape to them. Traditionally, employees have been submissive and employers have exercised dominance over them. The prevailing employee emotion in such relationships has been fear: fear of not getting a pay rise, fear of not getting promoted or simply fear of being out of a job and not eating.

So, traditionally, the boss has chosen those people he (or she) wanted in his team. The choice was with the boss. The potential employee had a limited choice: take the job or not. This was especially applicable in times when jobs were hard to come by. The family had to eat irrespective of how good or bad the boss was.

Times have changed. We now have Africa, Asia, the Americas, Australasia, Europe and effectively the globe within our reach for finding and filling jobs. In my travels within the UK it is a daily occurrence to encounter workers (professional or otherwise) from countries as far afield as Africa, Asia, Australia, the USA and Eastern Europe. In fact, Europeans are everywhere working in the UK. The guy who has just brought my PC back after it was struck down with a virus is from Macedonia.

**The guy who has just brought my PC back after it was struck down with a virus is from Macedonia.**

With international travel and globalization the job world has completely opened up. And with regular bouts of low unemployment the power has gradually shifted towards employees. Perhaps for the first time in the world's history employees have the freedom to choose where they work. It goes without saying that the type of work, location and pay are essential ingredients in any person's choice – but given an equal measure of these then a major factor influencing a person's choice is the boss and the company he works for.

There are too many horror stories springing out of the mires of low morale, demotivation, high attrition rates and industrial unrest to demonstrate that many people end up unhappy at work (and thus choose to leave) because of the approach taken by bosses and their companies.

So choose your boss *carefully*; he or she will have a major impact on your state of mind, your feelings and your future. You will normally have no more than one or at best two interviews to glean the information needed to make this essential choice. During these interviews your choice of microbehaviours will be critical in arriving at the most appropriate decision. The whole process of looking for a job (and thus a boss) is a long series of well-chosen microbehaviours, the outcome of which is the acceptance of a desired offer.

What to look for in a boss is worthy of a whole book. Here I will confine myself to ten essential factors. In the space of the interviews you will need to determine whether your future boss measures up against these ten factors (or whatever factors you choose).

The following paragraphs assume that it is your future boss who interviews you. In some organizations selection decisions are made by personnel departments who then assign successful candidates to bosses they do not know. In my opinion, this is an appalling practice. If you can at all avoid it do not work for these companies for the message is clear: they treat people like commodities and the bosses are not interested in you as a person (if they were they would be there at the interview).

## Choice factors

So here are some suggested choice factors for selecting a boss:

- He (or she) treats you like:
  - an equal
  - a human being
  - a person whom he cares for
  - a person who can be trusted
  - a person in whom he has total confidence
  - a person whom he really values
  - a person he likes

- He (or she) gives you all the time you need in helping you do your job effectively

- He (or she) takes a genuine interest in you as a person and demonstrates a genuine concern for your welfare and future

- He (or she) challenges you to do even better than you are currently doing – by encouraging you to undertake even more demanding tasks and attain even higher standards

- He (or she) is unstinting in his criticism of you when you fall below par and even more unstinting in his praise when you exceed expectations. In other words, he is totally honest with you about how he feels about your performance at work – and is prepared to give you negative feedback in the most positive of ways – to help you. He is also lavish in his praise – which is invariably spontaneous and comes from the heart

- He (or she) is totally open and transparent about everything. You know everything you need to know about what is going on – in the organization, in the team and in the boss's mind

- He (or she) is always pushing for you in other quarters, if not fighting for you. In other words, your boss is always on your side and attempts to balance this with the necessary requirements of the company. He pushes for you to get the promotions and transfers you and he think are appropriate – as well as fights to ensure that you receive a justified level of pay and awards. He also pushes for you to get any training that will benefit you (and thus the company)

- He (or she) is always firm and fair with you. He will not give in to your selfish demands and will not allow you to take advantage of his goodwill. He will always listen and try to understand but he will NOT say 'Yes' to you automatically. He will help you understand that he has to walk a tightrope, balancing the needs and interests of all team members together with that of the company

- He (or she) will put you at your ease. You will never feel uncomfortable in his presence (unless you have erred) and he will always welcome time spent with you. You will enjoy being with him and find it interesting, inspiring and motivating

- He (or she) will put you and other team members first. Thus if there is an exciting trip to be made to a foreign land he would rather have you make it on his behalf, should you so desire, than selfishly go himself. He will assign the highest priority of his time to you and the team. Should you have a problem he will drop everything to help you address this problem

I have been fortunate during my career to have had some excellent bosses who have measured up to many of these criteria. They have helped me along my way. They have been honest with me (when I erred) but have always pushed for me.

## Sensing these choice factors

When I sense these factors are in place then I do my best. I push for my bosses and I hate to let them down – because I know they will do their best not to let me down.

To choose the right boss you therefore need to develop effective microbe-haviours that sense other people's behaviour in relation to the factors you have in mind. Even choosing to put the appropriate sensing factors into your mind is a microbehaviour. The sensing process can be facilitated using 'yes/no' polarities, for example, 'yes, I sense he cares for people' as opposed to 'no, I sense he does not care'.

Once you have chosen to have these factors in mind you can sense compli-ance with these factors when the potential boss walks into the room. You can sense it by their attitude and the way they talk to you, take an interest in you, make eye contact with you. You can sense it by what they talk about and the priorities they give to various aspects of the job and the way it will be managed.

If you sense when walking in to an interview that the potential boss does not measure up then take care in making your choice. You could be leading yourself into a trap from which it is difficult to extricate yourself.

All of this applies to the interview situation when applying for a new job. If you are in an existing job and a new boss takes over the only choice you have is to determine whether or not the new boss measures up and, if not, to look for a transfer or leave. Whatever happens do not get stuck with a boss you hate; the negative emotion will eat away at you and destroy your life.

| BOX 12.1 | Application of the HOW method of choice |
|---|---|
| **H**esitate | Always give considerable second thoughts to the offer being put in front of you. Reflect on what you have experienced with your prospective new boss |
| **O**utcome | What do you project will be the outcome of working with this boss? How do you feel the relationship will evolve? Will it make both you and he feel as good as possible? |
| **W**ay | W-thinking: What other macro- and microbehavioural options do you have if you have a high degree of uncertainty about this potential new boss? Conversely, if you are attracted to working for this new boss what range of options do you have for developing an incredibly positive relation? |

**THE CHOICE CHALLENGE**

- When going for a job choose to interview your potential boss. Before the interview starts select the factors (ten examples given above) upon which you would choose to select your new boss.
- During the interview try to establish a balance of 'lead' – such that he (or she) leads the interview at certain stages and at other times you lead it. In this way you will be able to determine, using your predetermined factors, whether your potential boss is one of 'choice'.

# CHAPTER THIRTEEN

# Choosing how to communicate

## Managers have nothing else to do but communicate

### The activities managers undertake

Managers have nothing else to do but communicate. That is where all their energy goes. Such communication comprises a vast array of microbehaviours. Every movement of the eye, every gesture, every step taken, every phrase, every differentiating tone of voice, every look on the face is a communication microbehaviour which others observe and form opinions about. These opinions influence employees' behaviour and thus their motivation and performance. This is the work of managers: communication.

The other work requiring physical energy is done by frontline people who sweep floors, drive trucks, stack shelves, put up buildings, push paper, mend equipment, tend computers, poke at keyboards or serve customers. With rare exceptions (when they are trying to show off or 'muck in') managers do not use their muscles, in fact, all they do is talk or listen – often in that order of priority. Even when alone they talk to themselves.

Just reflect for a moment on the physical activities most managers undertake. Other than walking from one meeting to another they do nothing that requires hard work in the traditional sense of the word. All they do is sit in meetings, make phone calls, read documentation, write things down, send e-mails or dictate to others. The prime instruments of a manager's job are his mouth, eyes and ears, again normally in that order. Occasionally, the fingers are used too. Hidden behind these instruments is a brain and also, we hope, a heart and soul. Managers are therefore also meant to think for themselves as well as have a feel for others.

Many managers see their task as merely pushing paper (or electronic reports) around. This means receiving one document and adding a little to it before pushing it on to another person. This requires little energy and often (this is very evident) little skill.

These overt and obvious methods of communication (e.g. processing documents, making calls etc.) comprise a whole array of subsidiary microbehaviours which determine their effectiveness or otherwise.

Cynics would say that managers have another task and that is to get in the way of getting things done. They block things, holding them up pending a decision by someone else. These managers take energy out of the system by slowing things down, insisting on giving permissions for decisions better made by the people who have to implement them. (Isn't it irritating when you take a defective product back to the store where you bought it and the store assistant has to go and search for a supervisor to get permission to exchange the product or offer a refund?) These types of activity effectively display the negative microbehaviours of communication.

Ideally, managers get things done. They ease the way and facilitate the transition from the raw material in the hands of the supplier to the finished product in the hands of the customer. To accomplish this they devise systems. But systems are no more than devices for communication, for passing information around to trigger each stage of the operation. Say, for example, that an Area Manager employed by a retail chain receives the weekly sales figures for his various stores on a Monday. The first thing he does is read the figures (communication). He then thinks about them (talks to himself) and spots that one store is 20 per cent below plan. So he calls the store manager to ascertain (communication) what is happening. A discussion (communication) takes place resulting in a recovery plan. The store manager subsequently reports back (communicating) on progress. In other words the only thing a retail area manager does is communicate. Only rarely does he get on the shop floor and sell the products. It is not just WHAT a manager says in these situations but HOW a manager says it as well as WHY. The HOW and WHY aspects again comprise a vast number of communication microbehaviours.

**Ideally, managers get things done.**

# High- and low-level communication

At the high level of communications, managers therefore have to choose each of the following.

| CHOICE OF | |
|---|---|
| COMMUNICATION METHODS | (HOW) |
| REASONS FOR COMMUNICATION | (WHY) |
| WORDS AND MESSAGE | (WHAT) |

At the low level they have to choose the microbehaviours that comprise the how, why and what of communication.

Readers who think that managers do anything else but communicate should e-mail me at team@superboss.co.uk. I would be delighted to discover any activities that managers undertake which do not relate to communicating. Training is communication. Recruitment and selection is communication. Rewarding people is communication. Motivating people is communication. And, obviously, consultation and instruction is communication. So is listening and learning, questioning and challenging, nodding and grunting, smiling and frowning as well as cheering aloud or throwing your hands up in despair. Pinning paper on walls, inspecting various units and sitting at the computer is also communicating. It is all to do with the transmission, receipt and processing of information.

Much of this does, of course, depend on the quality of the communication and in which direction it flows. That is where CHOICE of microbehaviours comes in. The only discretion a manager has, in addition to spending money or allocating resources, is to CHOOSE the method of communication. In practical terms this means choosing between various methods of communication, as indicated in Box 13.1.

## BOX 13.1 Choice of high-level communication methods

|  | ONE WAY | THE OTHER WAY |
|---|---|---|
| MANAGER | →→→ | ←←← |
| e-mail message | Send | Receive |
| mobile (cellphone) | Call out | Receive call |
| office phone | —ditto— | —— ditto —— |
| document | Write | Read what others write |
| → traditional mail (external) | — ditto — | —— ditto —— |
| → memo/report (internal) | —ditto— | —— ditto —— |
| → fax | —ditto— | —— ditto —— |
| → e-mail | —ditto— | —— ditto —— |
| formal meetings (groups) | I speak they listen | They speak I listen |
| informal meetings (groups) | —— ditto —— | —— ditto —— |
| one-to-one meeting (interactive) | I initiate chat | He/she initiates chat |
| one-to-one meeting (instructive) | I tell | I am told |
| training | I lecture | I learn |
| study | I research | I read |
| time alone | I think (talk to my 'self') | I think ('self' talks to me) |
|  | (conscious to subconscious) | (subconscious to conscious) |

These are merely high-level choices. Within each activity is a further series of low-level choices as indicated in Box 13.2.

## BOX 13.2 Choice of low-level communication microbehaviours

| | | |
|---|---|---|
| intended outcome | tone of voice | words used |
| emotions revealed | degree of informality | wit/humour used |
| use of acronyms/jargon | gestures | eye contact |
| listening with intent | not listening | just hearing |
| listening with interest | attitude | anecdotal |
| polarities (yes/no inclination) | personal | impersonal |
| confiding | open/honest | closed |
| minimal | expansive | etc. |

It is quite apparent in many companies that many managers make the wrong communication choices both at high level (mechanisms) and at low level (macro- and microbehaviours). Employees just do not know what is going on, neither do they feel involved or consulted with. Often decisions are made without reasons being given and frequently people do not know where they stand. Praise is not given while criticism is liberal. These situations all reflect the choices managers make about communication.

The paradox is that while this author asserts that a manager's sole task is communication many managers are unaware of this and seem to give it little priority. They are, of course, communicating – but by default through their subconscious behaviours. Silence is a communication. It tells people things. Absence is a communication. It can create suspicion in people's mind. A look on a boss's face is a communication. In fact, virtually everything that goes on in an office is a communication – with the exception of cleaning windows and making the tea. On reflection, perhaps cleaning windows and making tea is communication. [Discuss.]

**Managerial problems stem from poor communication choices.**

The choice also extends to whom we do or do not communicate with. We can chat away to one person while completely ignoring another. We can give some important news to certain people while forgetting to do so for others.

Many managerial problems stem from poor communication choices.

## Application of the HOW method of choice

The method of choice can be applied to choosing how to communicate (Box 13.3).

| BOX 13.3 | Application of the HOW method of choice |
| --- | --- |
| **H**esitate | Think twice before you utter a word. Is there a better way? |
| **O**utcome | What is the purpose of this specific communication? What are you really trying to achieve with it? Will it make people feel as good as possible? |

**W**AY  W-thinking: Extend the range of macro- and microbehavioural options. What other communication options do you have? For example:

- Instead of writing should I telephone?
- Instead of telephoning should I go and see her?
- How long should I spend communicating?
- What is the ideal location for the communication?
- Are there are any better words I can use?
- Does this communication reflect my genuine beliefs? etc.

## E CHOICE CHALLENGE

- To be a great manager is to be a great communicator. It is your choice. The words, phrases, emotions and methods available to you are the same for every manager in the country. However, it is your choice of these which will set you apart from everyone else and distinguish you as a great boss.

# CHAPTER FOURTEEN

# Choosing to criticize

## All managers need to be critical

### In defence of criticism

Criticism is a much maligned and neglected art. Criticism is often construed as negativity and as such is suppressed. The

**Criticism is a much maligned and neglected art.**

long-term consequence of choosing NOT to criticize is to miss out on opportunities to move away from ineffective old ways into more effective new ways.

The biggest criticism thrown at people who criticize is that they put themselves across as knowing better than the other person. They set themselves up as paragons of virtue while projecting the deficiencies of those around them. Criticism is thus linked with arrogance and professions of superiority.

However, criticism is essential in life and the world would be a far worse place without it. Most managers fail at this neglected art. If I could criticize some managers for one thing it is that they do not criticize enough.

The cult of 'positive thinking' accompanied by 'positive strokes' and emphasis on 'feel good' factors means than rigorous criticism is out of fashion. It is not encouraged in textbooks or on training courses. The danger with positive thinking and positive strokes is that they encourage mediocrity and reinforce with praise and encouragement the ineptitude of the present approach while failing to expose the yawning deficiencies that most of us display in our daily performance. Positive stroking creates delusions of competence while good honest criticism exposes our personal limitations (which most of us are reluctant to accept).

As a result of this emphasis on the positive many managers, when they see something of which they do not approve, prefer not to criticize. They choose to look the other way, to tolerate low standards or to accept excuses. Others choose to criticize in ways that unintentionally make the situation worse and as such they gain reputations as ogres. 'There is no pleasing some!'

To criticize is to choose a critical behaviour, critical not only in the sense that it offers a criticism but also in the sense that this behaviour will have a critical impact on the long-term success of the other person as well as yourself.

Criticism is a behaviour that is incredibly difficult to use in relation to one-self. Self-criticism is a far inferior tool to that of having another criticize us. Despite what most of us think we cannot see ourselves for what we are unless another person holds up a mirror to our face. Many of us have distorted perceptions of ourselves and our own abilities: we think we know ourselves and we like to think that we know best and are doing our best. The reality is different and should be obvious from our frequent criticism of others – in fact most of us spend much of our lives criticizing others rather than criticizing ourselves.

Most sports stars have recognized this paradox and therefore welcome criticism. They hire coaches who criticize their game and suggest improvements. Sports stars know that they cannot win without someone criticizing them first. If they do not improve someone else will and they will lose. Criticism is thus essential for success in any walk of life. Sadly, most of us resist it and thus limit our performance to levels which others perceive as quite ordinary. Just walk into any store and witness the indifference and disinterest on the faces of most store assistants to experience ordinary service. Just ring any call centre and hear the drone of the voice at the other end (that is if you can get a human voice) to be subjected to the mediocrity of modern day customer relations. Nobody has criticized these people for their indifference, disinterest, droning voices and mediocrity.

As stated at the beginning of this chapter criticism is an art. Like any art it needs to be developed over a lifetime and, for any manager, over a career. It needs to be practised daily and with care. It needs to be practised to positive effect such that the outcome is motivation and steady improvement.

The choice to criticize must be founded on a set of critical principles held dear by the critic. These principles should form the basis of the art. My choice of critical principles would be as follows:

1  Set yourself exceptionally high standards

2  Be prepared to accept criticism yourself

3  Solicit criticism about yourself from others and learn from it

4  Only solicit criticism from experts you trust

5  Accept more criticism of yourself than you give to others

6  Agree with your team the exceptionally high standards that need to be kept

7  Only criticize others if you are an expert in the subject

8  Gain people's trust before you criticize them

9  Criticism must always be aimed at helping people

10  Criticism must always be focused on the high standards everyone agrees should be achieved

11  Criticism must never be aimed at hurting people

12  Criticism must never be personal (therefore must never be aimed at a person's heart, soul, spirit, self-identity, self-esteem, e.g. 'I don't like you because of what you have done')

13  Criticism must never be presented as a value judgement (e.g. 'you are absolutely useless')

14  Before you criticize show your love for the person you are criticizing

15  Remember your best friend is one who is prepared to criticize you

16  The purpose of your criticism should be clear to all: it should be directed at a more positive outcome (and thus eliminating deficiencies)

17  Balance every criticism with praise (for every piece of bad work there is always a piece of good work)

To quote Jack Welch at a presentation in London on 10 October 2001: 'The biggest job I have is to let people know how we feel about them. You have to tell them you love them and you have to kick them in the ass when they're not doing their job. And you got to be able to hug them and kick them in the ass frequently.'

Overall you should never choose to avoid criticism – either receiving it or giving it.

| BOX 14.1 | Application of the HOW method of choice |
|---|---|

**H**ESITATE    Always pause before criticizing. And then pause again.

**O**UTCOME    What am I really seeking to achieve by making this criticism? In what way will it make the other person feel good?

**W**AY    W-thinking: Extend the range of macro- and microbehavioural options. What other ways do I have of making this criticism? For example you might choose from the following:

- Is the criticism really necessary? Should I just ignore the situation that made me feel critical? (i.e. Should I be tolerant?)
- Should I just make a mental note then if the incident reoccurs that is when I will choose to express my critical view?
- Should I be spontaneous in expressing my criticism?
- Or should I take the person aside and make the criticism later?
- Should I e-mail the criticism or put it into writing?
- Should I choose to make a positive suggestion in offering the criticism?
- What words should I choose in making the criticism?
- What emotions should I express in making the criticism?
- Balancing your criticism with praise etc.

**E CHOICE CHALLENGE**

- For every criticism you make of another person it is essential that you receive one first and learn from it. It is this critical learning that will put you in the best position to criticize others.

# CHAPTER FIFTEEN

# Choosing emotions

## Every behaviour should be tagged with a positive emotion

### Emotional conversion

Emotion is all to do with motion. It moves us. Thus if we want to move in a certain direction we first have to choose the emotion. If we choose to be kind and compassionate we will move in the direction of caring for people. Conversely, if we choose to be forever angry (and I know quite a few people like this) then we will move in the direction of making frequent complaints.

**Emotion is all to do with motion. It moves us.**

To change ourselves and move in a better direction we therefore have to change our emotions and choose a better set. For example, I have just sent an e-mail off to an individual and back comes an automatic reply: 'I will be on vacation for the next two weeks (yippee!!!) and will reply to your e-mail on my return.' The choice of emotions in this case is clear. What the automatic reply did not say is: 'I will be on vacation for the next two weeks and I will reply to your e-mail on my return (yippee!!!).' This is, of course, perfectly understandable. For many people work generates negative emotions. It is seen as a chore and to be avoided if at all possible. People speak of that 'Monday morning feeling'. They look forward to the weekend when they do not have to work. Yippee!!!

This choice of negative emotions has a negative impact on people's work and thus on customers and the performance of the business. Far better the people who love to come to work and who take immense delight in serving their customers and who are proud of their company's success.

No work situation is so perfect that we cannot find cause for complaint. Conversely, no work situation is so bad that we cannot find cause for celebration. The cause we select is determined by the emotions we choose for ourselves.

If you wake up in the morning feeling bad about your boss then in all probability bad things will happen, thus making you feel even worse. It is a downward spiral. The problem is not that of your boss, but that of yourself. Conversely, if you wake up in the morning feeling good about your boss then there is a much higher probability that good things will happen. Thus our choice of emotions determines what happens to us. It effectively becomes a self-fulfilling prophesy. By choosing to be happy we generate happy behaviours which are then reciprocated by others. In other words, by choosing to be happy we attract towards ourselves situations which will make us even happier.

## Emotional choice

When confronted with any external situation the choice of emotion is ours. Yesterday I walked into Windsor to mail some letters. Before I reached the post office I went for a coffee. Then I remembered I had to go and buy a get well card for a friend. The walk into town takes between 20 and 30 minutes depending on the route I choose. On my return I had almost reached home when I realized I had not mailed the letters I had taken with me – and this was the original purpose of my journey! However, my other activities had distracted me and I had forgotten. I then had a choice – of emotions. I could choose to be angry with myself for having forgotten to mail the letters and the inconvenience a second journey would cause. Instead, I chose to be happy and welcomed the opportunity of a second walk into Windsor to mail the letters. Yesterday I walked twice the distance I normally do! What joy!

Most people who take a shower love the warm water. However, if the water suddenly turns ice cold many will scream blue murder: 'Who the hell has used all the hot water?' They choose to be angry. Conversely, I take delight in the ice-cold water, loving the way it stimulates my circulation and enables me to emerge with a glow. Our response is based solely on our choice of emotions.

As we go into the office every morning we need to choose our emotions carefully. The choice of the wrong emotions (or the choice of no emotions) will have a deleterious effect on our team. However, if we choose to love our team and show delight in seeing them then the positive emotions we reveal will have an incredibly positive impact on their motivation. It is not good enough to justify our bad moods by saying, 'I have to be true to myself – and if this is the way I feel then this is the way I have to be.' Being true to ourselves does not mean caving in to the bad feelings we all experience from time to time – but actually choosing to replace them with good feelings. If we want to be good and thus feel good we must choose good emotions. Some of the positive emotions from which we can choose can be found in Box 15.1.

| BOX 15.1 | Positive emotions | | | |
|---|---|---|---|---|
| enjoyment | happiness | joy | relief | contentment |
| bliss | delight | amusement | pride | thrill |
| satisfaction | acceptance | friendliness | trust | kindness |
| affinity | devotion | adoration | elation | compassion |
| understanding | love | excitement | empathy | warmth |

Similary, as managers, our aim should be to stimulate positive emotions in our teams such they generally feel good about coming to work. We will need to work hard to generate the following feelings among our people (Box 15.2).

| BOX 15.2 | More positive emotions | |
|---|---|---|
| feeling valued | feeling appreciated | feeling trusted |
| feeling respected | feeling supported | feeling understood |
| feeling challenged | feeling excited | feeling happy |
| feeling important | feeling involved | feeling inspired |
| feeling welcomed | feeling free (to take initiatives) | feeling responsible |

To have this impact requires choosing positive emotions to drive our behaviours and thus relationships with our team and our own bosses as well as with our customers.

Everything we do, whether it is a microbehaviour, a big decision, or a simple communication with another person presents you with a choice of emotions.

You will need to choose which emotions you attach (or tag) to any communication or behaviour:

- a positive emotion (e.g. a tone of voice expressing kindness)

- a negative emotion (e.g. a tone of voice expressing irritation)

- no emotion (e.g. a matter of fact tone of voice)

This choice of emotions will have a major impact on your future success especially in terms of how you develop and maintain the essential relations with customers, suppliers, colleagues, bosses and acquaintances.

| BOX 15.3 | Application of the HOW method of choice |
|---|---|
| **H**esitate | When other people are involved always get in touch with your heart before you do anything and determine how you feel about the situation |
| **O**utcome | Identify the emotions you want these other people to feel as a result of whatever you intend to do. Ideally these should be positive emotions |
| **W**ay | W-thinking: Extend the range of macro- and microbehavioural options. Having identified how you feel about the current situation explore what other emotional options you have in addition to the instinctive one of reflecting your immediate feelings. For example, you might choose from the following: |

- Give some spontaneous expression to how you feel (whether it be negative or positive) *(e.g. 'I feel angry the way you screwed up on this')*

- Supplement a negative emotion with a positive one *(e.g. 'You know I value the hard work you have undertaken for us recently but I thought I ought to let you know how I feel about the way you handled this situation - I wasn't happy at all')*

- Eliminate the negative emotion *(e.g 'It's happened. Let's forget it and move on')*
- Find a different emotion to express yourself (in this case empathy) *(e.g. 'This happened to me when I started out too. I really understand how you feel but on reflection you will discover that this was a great lesson. You will be a better person for it')*
- Find a different emotion to express yourself (in this case appreciation and reassurance) *(e.g. 'I am delighted you made a decision. It is far better than not making a decision. Do not worry that it did not work out on this occasion')*

## THE CHOICE CHALLENGE

- Choose to add a degree of positive emotion to everything you do and say. Then reserve negative emotions for the odd occasion when they can be used to make a positive impact.

# CHAPTER SIXTEEN

# Choosing expertise

## To be successful it is essential that a manager focus on his or her desired area of expertise and develop it

### The need for developing expertise

One of my favourite provocations, especially when speaking to education-alists, is to say: 'I learnt nothing at school – except how to pass exams.' I then go on to say: 'In fact I am the world's leading expert in passing exams – having obtained a degree and a PhD. The reason I am here speaking with you today is all to do with what I have learned in the "University of Life" – and very little to do with what I learned at school and at university.'

I exaggerate, of course. Formal classroom education is vitally important in helping people develop IMPERSONAL skills and knowledge relating to such subjects as engineering, science, medicine, law and even languages. However, formal classroom education is less useful in developing PER-SONAL skills and knowledge.

While it is possible for a professor to prescribe all the IMPERSONAL skills and knowledge you need to be an expert in computing, chemistry, cardiol-ogy or Chinese cryptography there is not a single body of accepted expert-ise that prescribes the essential PERSONAL skills and knowledge required for individual effectiveness in any one job, let alone in relationships.

Divorce is rampant in our modern society. I myself have been married twice. However, it is not as if, before a wedding, a young couple have to attend classroom tuition in modern marriage, read textbooks on the subject, prac-tise marriage in the laboratory and then pass an examination with an 'A' or

'B' grade before being qualified to commit at a wedding ceremony. Some might argue that this would be a good course of education for most engaged couples. In reality, the development and conduct of any relationship cannot be prescribed by an educational syllabus taught in a classroom. Relationship skills is just one area of expertise that many managers neglect to develop.

**Relationship skills is just one area of expertise that many managers neglect to develop.**

To be successful it is essential that we focus in on our desired areas of expertise and develop them.

## Developing unique expertise

In a competitive world it is no good relying on skills and knowledge prescribed by professors to develop this expertise, after all, these taught skills and knowledge are equally available to our competitors. The essence of success is to develop a degree of expertise that other people do not have. It is our choice of such unique expertise that will set us apart and make us valuable. The uniqueness of this expertise needs to be developed continually. You can even develop unique relationship skills (icons of success like Sir Richard Branson exhibit unique relationship skills).

Our choices in developing expertise, both personal and impersonal, will depend on our daily behaviours and our choices of what to learn and how. When we get home we have many choices – we can watch television, play with the kids or read a book. Or we can note down in an exercise book our experiences and learn from this. Or we can go and have a drink with the experts and learn from them. There are 1,000 different ways of developing our expertise – but each starts with our own individual choices of microbehaviours. It goes on from there.

But first we need to focus on our desired expertise. My wife Mechi is an expert linguist; I am not. She is always developing her expertise – by practising the various languages she speaks (Spanish, English, French, Italian etc.) and mixing with people who speak these languages. Our previous next door neighbour was a cardiologist who developed (and continued to develop) an immense expertise in the (impersonal) workings of the heart as well as in relationship skills. His patients love him – and that is from the heart, they trust him, respect him and just know that he does his very best for them.

Doing our best is a reflection of the expertise we have. The more expert we become the better we can do.

Unless we choose to develop our expertise, whatever it is, we put ourselves at risk from competitors who have developed a higher degree of expertise –which customers and employers will value more.

Any manager therefore, to stay ahead, has continually to develop his expertise both in the IMPERSONAL side of the business but also with respect to his PERSONAL skills and knowledge. The latter is often much neglected.

Developing expertise to stay ahead does not come easy. Learning by design is far preferable to learning by accident. The choice is yours:

- What is your expertise?
- Do you really want to become an expert in the chosen topic(s)?
- What have you learnt today to improve your expertise?
- What steps will you be taking over the next few days to develop your expertise?
- What changes can you make to your lifestyle and method of working to exhibit expertise?

I visit many hot countries where I have a tendency to get through three shirts a day. This means I sometimes bring home over 20 shirts to be washed and ironed. We used to have an excellent woman who came to iron my shirts but she recently moved with her husband to another part of the country. So my wife found another woman to help us out. Unfortunately she was not so good – despite a fair amount of guidance she seemed unable to fold the shirts the way I liked. Furthermore, sometimes the collars came out a little crinkled and on rare occasions there was a scorch mark on the tail of the shirt. So now we have found another ironing woman and she is much better. She is an expert in ironing shirts and also has excellent relationship skills.

In other words, whatever our job, whether it be ironing shirts, cleaning streets or chief executive of a major corporation, there are always opportunities to develop our expertise. It is our choice to create and seize them. In fact the development of our IMPERSONAL expertise (ironing shirts) is dependent on the development of our PERSONAL expertise (listening, learning and taking guidance). When we fail to develop our personal expertise the probability is we will fail in developing our impersonal expertise.

I try to learn something new every day. In that way I try to sustain my expertise and push back the boundaries. For example, I am now reading a thought-provoking book, *Fooled by Randomness*, by Nassim Nicholas Taleb. It has taught me something new about the random nature of success. Last week I was reading *Driven* by Paul Lawrence and Nitin Nohra from which I learnt something new about how our genes influence our motivational drives. In between I have been reading the biography of the late poet Ted Hughes by Elaine Feinstein. I learnt a lot from Feinstein's description of his relationship with Sylvia Plath.

Ten days ago I wrote a letter to Rod Eddington, Chief Executive of British Airways complimenting Jack Stevenson, a member of BA's cabin crew who had given me excellent service on a flight to Singapore. I have received a personal reply from Rod Eddington. I learn from this. The personal reply makes me feel good – and I also wanted Jack Stevenson and Rod Eddington to feel good.

In addition, I have also written to three other chief executives recently expressing compliments. They have chosen not to reply. You can learn from this too. What I have learnt is that if Rod Eddington cares enough to reply personally to a customer then I will take care to fly British Airways in the future. As for the chief executives who chose not to reply to my letters of compliments, then I have learnt to care less for their organizations. Forget them! That is the lesson.

Such small behaviours (whether or not to reply personally to a customer) are all part of the expertise senior executives develop. In turn Jack Stevenson, the Cabin Services Director with British Airways, has developed a special expertise that I rarely find on other airlines. He knows how to make customers feel good: 'I advise my crews that I want people to board the 747 as customers and leave as friends.' That is his wisdom, his expertise and he applies it throughout a flight. I learn from that.

# The choice of expertise

The choice of expertise is all important. I do not want to have the same expertise as all my competitors – I want to have something unique. So I work hard in developing that unique expertise – and this means making conscious choices every day on how to develop it. These choices relate to the books and journals I read, the television programmes I occasionally watch, the films I go to see with my wife – as well as the concerts we attend and the people I initiate relationships with. And, by the way, I have learnt more from street cleaners than I have from many managers!

Ultimately, the best way to choose the areas in which we wish to become expert is to identify areas of our work and life which genuinely interest us. For example, I am genuinely interested in customer relationships with specific reference to the psychology of interaction that takes place between an employee and customer. I have therefore studied hundreds of books on the subject, attended conferences, listened to and met the experts (not always the self-proclaimed experts – but more frequently the practitioners) as well as initiated research to gain experience and learn from it. Furthermore, I am an avid reader of over 20 different professional journals. There is nothing magic in this approach to developing my expertise – I just focus on this area and aim continually to develop my expertise by working hard at pushing back the boundaries of my own skills and knowledge.

As mentioned earlier a second key factor in developing expertise relates to curiosity and one's desire to question and challenge. Curiosity is closely aligned with interest in a certain topic. We should therefore seek out situations which embrace this topic and then learn from the experience, being curious about what happens in that situation and questioning all involved. Thus if we encounter an expert we should seize the opportunity, even if we only have a minute with this person, to ask some pertinent question. Furthermore, we should make choices to seek out experts for an exchange of experiences. At worst they will say 'no'. Often they will say 'yes' and we will learn.

| BOX 16.1 | Application of the HOW method of choice |
| --- | --- |

**H**esitate      Reflect on your UNIQUE expertise. What is it and in what way is it UNIQUE? What have you learnt recently to enhance that expertise?

**O**utcome      Set yourself a challenge to develop that uniqueness every day. Learn something new today and record the outcome. It will make you feel good and benefit others too

**W**ay      W-thinking: Extend the range of macro- and microbehavioural options. Explore new ways of extending the UNIQUENESS of your expertise. Expose yourself to unusual situations, do different things and discover how this can help you

The 2001 Turner Prize for Art was awarded to Martin Creed at the Tate Britain Art Gallery. His prize-winning exhibit was a light switching on and off in a large room with white walls. His other works of art include a crumpled ball of paper and a piece of Blu-Tack stuck on a wall

I can assure you that I have learnt from this (about pushing back boundaries) and my expertise has been enhanced as a result

What options are you creating and exploiting to develop your expertise?

### THE CHOICE CHALLENGE

- Push back the boundaries of your expertise every day of your life. So choose to learn something new in this area today, tomorrow and every day thereafter. Become unique by having UNIQUE expertise.

# CHAPTER SEVENTEEN

# Choosing eye contact

## People reveal themselves through their eyes

### The microbehaviour of eye contact

Most times eye contact is controlled subconsciously. We are hardly aware that we turn our face and avoid the look in another person's eyes. We are hardly aware that when someone is talking to us our gaze is elsewhere.

Eye contact creates an emotional connection through which the power of deep-rooted personal energies is transmitted. For many there is an entrenched fear that when someone catches our eye we will reveal too much and they will see too much. For others eye contact creates a vulnerability to predatory forces, sometimes sexual, sometimes commercial and sometimes vindictive.

Conversely, those people who exude a high degree of confidence put themselves in a position of power by initiating eye contact. These are the people with a 'dominant' eye. Weaker brethren tend to have 'submissive' eyes.

In a hierarchy eye contact reveals your position. In the ancient courts nobody would dare initiate eye contact with the emperor for fear of the worst. Eye contact equals intimacy and in certain societies only the closest members of your family and circle of friends would get to look into your eyes. I have visited Saudi Arabia innumerable times and have yet to make eye contact with a woman from that country.

Eye contact is complex. When the teacher asks a question most pupils will stare down at their desks, avoiding the teacher's gaze. Only the brightest will catch the teacher's eye to answer the question. We have all looked the other way at times, when we see people approaching we do not want to see. We pretend not to notice. We avoid their eyes as if they were not there.

Nobody wants to be caught out and it is through the eyes that we get caught out. Intentions get declared and suspicions exposed through the eyes. We see the child eyeing the candy, the husband eyeing the

**We hide ourselves by avoiding eye contact.**

pretty woman. It is all too easy to read people's minds by looking into their eyes. So we hide ourselves by avoiding eye contact. It is as if we wanted to put a veil over our eyes.

In the world of retail an angry customer is a customer with angry eyes. We all recognize those eyes and our inclination, subconsciously, is to avoid that threat, to avoid the potential aggression. So we look away, naively hoping that the problem will go away – because we are looking away.

Conversely, we are attracted to smiling eyes or at least eyes which exhibit a genuine smile. There are hundreds of ways of smiling and it is the minutiae of eye movements that reveal the type of smile. It could be a false smile, a wry smile, an insincere smile, a warm smile, a funny smile, an angry smile, a friendly smile or one of many other types of smile – each revealed through the merest inflection of eye movement and facial expression. We do not have time to think about the look on another's face or the look we are giving them. The look, the smile, the eye movement are mostly automatic and driven by the power of our subconscious.

If it is eyes that give us away then it is eyes that have the power to put us on the road to success. Through our eyes we control our destiny – by seeing what we want to see and avoiding what we do not want to see. If we see other people as being a major factor in helping us along the road to success then it is our eyes that will have to do the work initially in establishing the all-important relationships.

Simply put, people do not want to do business with others who avert their gaze. Eyes create value. When there is eye contact the message can be, 'You are so important that I am giving you my full attention.' When there is no eye contact the message is, 'You are not important to me.' This essential rule (of the value of eye contact) is much neglected. We will return to the restaurant where the waitress caught our eye while avoiding the restaurant where we could catch the eye of no one. We value people who catch our eye.

Bosses promote people who catch their eye while customers prefer the shops that catch their eye.

To catch someone's eye and put ourselves on the road to success we have to learn to make eye contact. This means making conscious choices about the microscopic movements we make with our eyes. We have to become conscious of what is happening to our eyes – as well as that of others.

Thus, in choosing to make eye contact with another person we have first to choose what part of our self we intend to reveal to them. Do we intend to reveal our love through our eyes, our curiosity, our interest or (on the reverse side) our irritation or anger? Do we reveal or hide our ulterior motives when we look at another person? We have to choose between a glance, a gaze, a stare, a look, a nod, a wink or an intense communicative connection. And then we have to choose whether the glance or stare is warm or cold, friendly or hostile.

Overall, it is best to make honourable eye contact with as many people as physically possible in any one day. It will be hard work because an immense amount of emotional energy will be streaming through our eyes. However, in the end all this hard work on eye contact will pay dividends. Over a period of time we will create relationships, arising from our initial eye contact, which will be mutually beneficial. By choosing to avoid eye contact with all but our closest friends and family we restrict ourselves to a small relationship circle and thus deny ourselves all manner of possibilities as well as exposing ourselves to the risk of limited help in times of trouble.

| BOX 17.1 | Application of the HOW method of choice |
|---|---|

| | |
|---|---|
| **H**esitate | When you are with another person (or group of people) try to create a conscious awareness of what is happening to your eyes |
| **O**utcome | Determine what you want to communicate through your eyes and the desired outcome |
| **W**ay | W-thinking: Extend the range of microbehavioural options. Examine the possibilities of what you can do with your eyes in any given encounter. For example, you might choose from the following: |

- Do my eyes show DELIGHT when I meet a stranger?
- Do my eyes show COMPASSION when someone brings me a problem?
- Do my eyes show INTEREST in what the person is talking about (or do they wander indicating DISINTEREST)?
- Do my eyes SPARKLE? (or are they dull?)
- Do my eyes show APPRECIATION or lack of it? etc.

## THE CHOICE CHALLENGE

- Catch someone's eye at least five times a day.
- Then let other people catch your eye at least ten times a day.

# CHAPTER EIGHTEEN

# Choosing first steps

## Take a different step every morning

### An infinite number of possibilities

Your morning routine should be far from routine. It presents an infinite number of possibilities from which to choose. The choices you make will set the tone for the day and have an indirect but substantial impact on what happens during the day.

When in automatic mode you always choose the same way to travel to work, always leaving at the same time, driving the same route, catching the same train or parking in the same place. When you step out of automatic mode you start thinking about the possibilities which can affect your life. David Alleston, a regional operations manager with the shoe retailer Stead and Simpson, always parks on the far side of the car park, choosing the furthest distance to walk. He rarely uses elevators, preferring always to walk up the stairs. These are unusual but conscious choices. You only have to visit any car park to see where the majority of people choose to park – and that is as close to the entrance as possible.

When you arrive at your desk you also have an infinite number of choices. Here are a few:

1  You can close the door

2  You can leave the door open

3  You can grab a coffee and read the morning paper

4  You can pull out the company's statement of values and challenge yourself on how you are going to put them into practice today

5   You can switch on your PC and check your e-mail

6   You can tap into the PC and check on yesterday's financial results

7   You can start making calls to colleagues from your mobile

8   You can start making calls to customers to find out how things are

9   You can go through your in-tray

10   You can prepare for a meeting later that morning

11   You can start immediately with a formal meeting (previously scheduled)

12   You can walk the floor and spend half an hour chatting to whoever's in

13   You can walk the floor and spend five minutes chatting to whoever's in

14   You can walk the floor and choose to take an interest in the people there, enquiring about their wellbeing

15   You can walk the floor and consult people on your own agenda of topics

16   You can go and see your boss

17   You can ring each member of your team to check on progress made on the tasks you set them yesterday (or the week before)

18   You can go and see each member of your team to check on progress made on the tasks you set them yesterday (or the week before)

19   You can lie on the floor and meditate

20   You can spend five minutes reading from your favourite business book in order to obtain a fresh stimulus for the day and to energize you

The choice is yours. The possibilities are infinite. Whatever choice you make with respect to your first step every morning, you can rest assured it will have an impact on the rest of the day and the overall performance of you and your team. The reason is that each choice you make will reflect your own personal values and the outcomes you wish to accomplish. Thus, if you place an immense amount of value on having a happy motivated team then the first steps you take each morning will reflect this. Similarly, if you place an immense amount of value on achieving exceptional financial figures day by day then the first steps you take each morning will reflect this.

**Whatever choice you make with respect to your first step every morning will have an impact on the rest of the day and the overall performance of you and your team.**

In other words, the first steps you take each morning will reflect your choices about what is important to you. Each of these steps is a microbehaviour that is effectively a microcosm of your approach to work.

| **BOX 18.1** | **Application of the HOW method of choice** |
|---|---|

**H**esitate    Before you go to bed reflect on the first steps you intend to take tomorrow morning at work. Then reflect again on this as you journey to work

In considering your first step each morning ask yourself the following questions:

1 What do I really want to achieve in my first half-hour at work every morning?

2 What is really important to me when I arrive at work in the morning? What do I value?

3 What is going to make me feel good when I arrive at work in the morning?

4 What are the activities that I undertake first thing at work which will have a substantial impact on the accomplishment of the outcomes I desire and the principles I wish to apply over the longer term?

**O**utcome    Set yourself a challenge. What is the first thing you want to achieve this morning to make other people feel good (and also yourself feel good)?

**W**ay    W-thinking: Extend the range of microbehavioural options. Review the list of 20 steps and amend it as you think appropriate. Then choose a first step which is different to any first step you have taken over the last four weeks.

Here are some further examples of microbehavioural choices you might make using 'YES/NO' polarities:

● Schedule a formal meeting right at the beginning of the day (YES/NO)

● Arrive 30–60 minutes before the first formal meeting (YES/NO)

● Spend 5–30 minutes chatting informally with the team (YES/NO)

- Enter the office and close the door (YES/NO)
- Enter the office and leave the door open (YES/NO)
- Walk around before entering the office (YES/NO)
- Start making calls (YES/NO)
- Check and reply to e-mail (YES/NO)
- Go through your paperwork (YES/NO)
- Do something unusual (YES/NO) like meditate or read a book or listen to music

## THE CHOICE CHALLENGE

- The first step you take every morning is a further step on your route to success or failure; there is no going back on that.

# CHAPTER NINETEEN

# Choosing to be happy

## Happiness is a choice

### How to make yourself happy

Every morning Richard Killoran travels into Central London to work as General Manager of Austin Reed's flagship store at Piccadilly. Every morning as he stands there on the underground train, squashed up against other commuters he counts up to ten things which make him happy. He tells himself: 'I have a beautiful wife, a lovely home and a nice car. I am fit and well and I've just had a great vacation in the south of France. Furthermore, I've got a job I enjoy. I work with a fantastic team of people and I love the customers who come into the store. I have a really good boss and have benefited from a good career progression during my working life. The products we sell in the store are first class and overall we are doing well relative to plan.'

Having chosen to be happy he bounces into the store every morning a happy man. That makes his team happy as well as his customers.

Happiness is a choice. Each one of us can choose to be happy or we can choose to be miserable. If I wake up in the morning and I choose to feel bad about my wife then bad things will happen. However, my wife, Mechi, has many beautiful qualities and I love her dearly. Therefore, I choose to wake up in the morning feeling good about my wife. I always look for the good things in her – and there are so many. By choosing to feel good about my wife I virtually guarantee that good things will happen in our relationship.

The same principle can be applied to work. If you choose to be happy coming to work then things will occur which will make you and others happy. Conversely, if you choose (or accidentally allow yourself) to be miserable then it is virtually guaranteed that things will occur which will reinforce your misery.

Heinrich Grafe who runs the Conrad International Centennial Hotel in Singapore informs his staff: 'I only have one job and that is to ensure you are happy. When you are happy our customers will be happy too. If for any reason you feel unhappy before coming to work then it's best you do not come to work that day.'

Happiness arises from looking for and finding the good things in our lives. Anybody reading this book will not be so deprived that they cannot find good things in their lives. In other words, there is always a reason to feel happy; we just have to choose that reason and be happy.

**Happiness arises from looking for and finding the good things in our lives.**

It is so easy to focus on the negative, on the problems, on the things that go wrong in our lives (and in the world around us) and as a consequence put ourselves into an unhappy frame of mind. But that is effectively our choice – and that choice will be reflected in our behaviours, on our relationships and on the results we achieve.

Admittedly none of us can escape moments of unhappiness. There will be times when loved ones die, when accidents occur, when disease afflicts us, when chaos reigns, when disasters blow up in our face (September 11 2001, for example). During these crises our emotions may dip to an incredibly low level. However, we cannot allow them to remain there forever. Queen Victoria was criticized by the British nation for grieving for too long after the death of her beloved husband, Albert, in December 1861. She grieved for almost ten years and for periods became a virtual recluse. It took the notorious John Brown to help elevate her from her gloom and return to a more normal happy state.

John Spence, a senior executive with the UK bank Lloyds TSB, is blind. He is a great character and gives hilarious and inspirational talks. He is fond of saying, 'The best thing that ever happened to me was to go blind.' Lance Armstrong, the champion cyclist, was given a one in five chance of living when he was diagnosed as having cancer. After being treated with chemotherapy and fighting the disease he returned to his beloved sport and won the Tour de France. In his book[1] he states: 'Cancer was the best thing that happened to me. It did wonders for me.' Tony Bullimore, who was entrapped in a lightless air pocket when his yacht capsized in icy storm-ridden seas, stated:[2] 'I survived because I wanted to, I had no intention of going down in the Southern ocean. It's amazing what you can achieve when you put your mind to it.'

Happiness is a broad set of positive emotions which we prise out of our heart with a selection of conscious stimuli. Happiness is not necessarily a product of our current state of physical comfort or discomfort. Pain does not automatically lead to unhappiness and neither does pleasure automatically lead to happiness. The person who experiences the momentarily pleasing physical sensations of alcohol can often be a very unhappy person.

In other words, we choose our state of mind (our mindset) and we choose our set of emotions (our heartset) and it is both of these that drive our behaviours.

Earlier today I was walking along the riverside at Windsor (where I live) with my wife and daughters. I felt good and said to myself, 'It's great to be alive.' That was happiness. The sun was out, people were feeding the swans, families were enjoying picnics while there were many tourists admiring the view of the Windsor Castle above us and Eton College on the other side of the Thames. My family and I had just been enriched by a most convivial lunch at Puccino's. Our waitress Nicky even refused our offer of a tip. 'You're friends,' she told us. 'I don't like to accept tips from friends.' Happiness: Nicky was happy, her bosses Tony and Mary-Jo Brompton were happy and as a result their customers were happy. Friendly customer service means having friends and being happy to see them.

As a boss if you walk into work every morning happy to see your team then there is a high probability they will be happy. Their happiness is your choice and reflects your own happiness. One store assistant in London told me, 'Our boss is very moody. Sometimes she is bubbling, smiling and cheerful – and that's when we are happy. We like to see her happy. Other times she goes into the director's office and comes out looking tense and stressed.

She will have a permanent frown on her face. We will sense something is wrong and that will make us unhappy.'

How we respond to things going wrong is our choice. When we perceive other people to be behaving badly or when we do not get our own way it is all too easy to allow ourselves to become unhappy – with a consequential impact on others. In my training workshops I often notice that the people who complain the most about their bosses and the organization as a whole are those who generally have a miserable disposition – while their colleagues who are happy (including those working for the self-same bosses and organization) rarely complain. It is a choice. If your boss shouts at you the choice is yours: you can become unhappy as a result or remain happy.

| BOX 19.1 | Application of the HOW method of choice |
|---|---|
| **H**esitate | Spend a few moments thinking about all the things in your life that make you happy |
| **O**utcome | Make 'happiness' your word for today and aim to end the day having made at least one other person happy as well as yourself |
| **W**ay | W-thinking: Extend the range of macro- and microbehavioural options for being happy. What additional choices can you make today which will result in increased happiness for all around? Here are some examples. You could choose to: |

1 Reflect on all the good things in your life
2 Reflect on all the good things in your work (and express it to others)
3 Look for and find good things about other people
4 Show you are happy in everything you do (every micro-behaviour)
5 Give a kind word
6 Give a word of praise
7 Produce an extra smile
8 Take an interest in someone
9 Buy a small gift and present it nicely
10 Discuss 'what makes us happy' at the team meeting (this will make you far happier than discussing problems)

**11** Do something special for another person today

**12** Find out something interesting about each person you meet today

**13** Dismiss from your mind anything that makes you unhappy

**14** Try to agree with each person you meet

**15** Say 'yes' to other people's request and only use 'no' as a last resort

**16** Enjoy other people's company

**17** Make someone laugh

**18** Find something that will make you smile

**19** Listen to music

**20** Admire the flowers

**21** Admire another person

**22** Listen to another person

**23** Learn something new

**24** Show enthusiasm for other people's ideas

**25** Go round saying 'thank you' with good reason

**26** Whistle, hum or sing (but not for too long!)

## HE CHOICE CHALLENGE

● Sit back and reflect on all those good things in your life which make you happy and then choose to be happy.

## Notes

**1** *It's Not About the Bike* by Lance Armstrong, Yellow Jersey Press, 2000

**2** *Saved* by Tony Bullimore, Little, Brown & Co, 1997

# CHAPTER TWENTY

# Choosing to initiate relationships

## All long-term relationships start with the briefest of encounters

### Some indisputable facts

Fact 1  It is impossible to have a relationship, of any kind, with every single person in this world

Fact 2  It is impossible to have a relationship with every person we encounter in life. The majority of people pass in and out of our lives without any emotional connection which might spark a relationship

Fact 3  It is possible to have relationships with many more people than we currently do. It is simply a matter of personal choice

Fact 4  Personal relationships are a critical factor in determining the successes we experience in life. Our choice of success is therefore dependent on our choice of personal relationships

Fact 5  There are two types of relationships:
– Strong relationships (family, close friends, long-standing colleagues)
– Weak relationships (acquaintances)

It is these 'weak' relationships that we will focus on in this section. They are critical in determining the progress we make in life. To make progress in our careers as managers it is therefore important to extend our circle of 'weak' relationships, as illustrated in Figure 20.1.

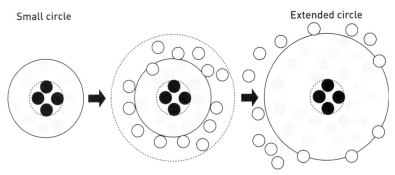

○ New acquaintances *(no relationships extending to weak relationships)*

Existing acquaintances *(weak relationships)*

● Close members of our personal inner circle *(strong relationships)*

**Figure 20.1**   Extending the circle of relationships: Our personal choice

Strong relationships require an immense amount of time and personal energy to sustain. They serve a vital purpose in promoting and sustaining intimate levels of personal interest, understanding, mutual respect and mutual support. However, strong relationships are not conducive to managerial success. With only twenty-four hours in every day it is impossible to devote sufficient time to sustain a close relationship with most colleagues, employees, customers and suppliers. Even if a manager spent one hour a week in individual communication and consultation with his closest business partners this would limit him to a maximum inner circle of 60 people (assuming a 60-hour working week). Strong relationships, therefore, are confined to members of families with whom we like to spend a lot of time and a handful of very close friends with whom we are happy to spend hours (whether out on the golf course, in the pub or down at the community centre).

It is not our close friends who are going to give us our best business leads or introduce us to the innumerable contacts we need to extend our network. Involving close friends in our business puts them at risk of having to let us down and thus erode the strong relationship we have with them.

Business success is therefore built on weak relationships where the time devoted to a relationship might be no more than five minutes in two years. Yet the choice to spend five minutes in two years with one person as

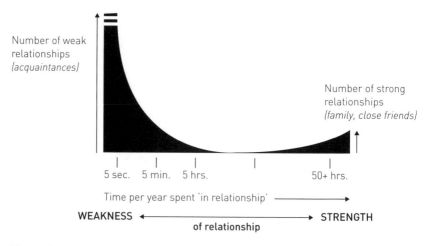

**Figure 20.2**   Strength of relationships

opposed to another is critically important in the long-term success of the business. Without that five minutes there would be no relationship and a risk the business would suffer as a result (see Figure 20.2).

It is not a matter of choosing between weak and strong relationships. All long-term relationships start with the briefest of encounters. It is a matter of choosing to establish a relationship with as many people as possible such that they become memorable as opposed to fading away. When a positive memory of a brief five-minute encounter remains in the mind a relationship is formed. Too many people pass through our lives without our even remembering them.

**Too many people pass through our lives without our even remembering them.**

In choosing to establish a relationship we are therefore making a choice during the first minute we spend with a person (in whatever the circumstance) between treating that person like an inanimate object (as if they were a number) or like a human being. To do the latter we attempt to spark an emotional connection between two hearts, thus striking up a relationship, no matter how momentary. As soon as we turn off the heart it is not possible to establish this connection. The end result of this turn-off is a perception of indifference, apathy, neglect and rejection (as a human being). When this happens the interaction becomes impersonal and the other person feels they are being treated as if they were a number.

This turn-off is prevalent in companies that are task driven. They tend to treat employees like robots, instructing them to follow systems and procedures and programming them with the appropriate training. In these task-driven companies the transaction becomes a thousand times more important than the customer requiring it. By failing to establish weak relationships they effectively dehumanize their customers, their employees and their business as a whole. They become heartless and grind their employees and customers through a giant organization machine which churns out revenue and profit at the least possible cost.

It is a personal choice. In all probability our long-term success will be accomplished as a result of the extensive circle of weak relationships we have established in life, not because of our close friends. We never know the future and thus will not know what part that person we spend five minutes with today will play in our future. However, if we choose not to initiate contact and therefore not to spend five minutes it is highly probable that that person will play no further positive part in our future.

In making our personal choices about whom to initiate 'weak' relationships with we must follow our hearts. We are more likely to establish such a relationship if we 'like' a person, after all the basic motivational driver in our lives is that we move towards situations and people that make us feel good and move away from situations and people that make us feel bad. We will therefore initiate relationships with people we like, who make us feel good. We will sense this immediately they enter the room.

You might argue that it is impossible to like everyone in this world and therefore we are quite justified in avoiding initiating relationships with people we dislike. This is our choice. However, one of our extended W-thinking options is not to reject a person because we do not like them but to go seeking things about them we do like. In doing so we will connect with more people and establish many more relationships.

In other words, in choosing to initiate a relationship with another person we need to choose something we like about that person – and this will form the basis of the relationship. Overall, the more people we like, the more relationships we will have and the more successful we will become in life. Try it now!

I am forever quoting Jack Welch, but one factor contributing to his success over 20 years was his ability to form weak relationships with tens of thousands of people. To quote from his book *Jack*:

**❝I didn't want to be a picture in the annual report. I wanted to be someone whom everyone in GE knew. [Bear in mind that General Electric has hundreds of thousands of employees.] At Crotonville [GE's management training centre] I've led exchanges with more than 18,000 managers over the last twenty years.❞**

Earlier he states: 'The job of a CEO is close to 75 per cent about people and 25 per cent about other stuff.'

Each of those 18,000 managers will have a story to tell about Jack Welch and will feel they have a relationship with him, no matter how weak. It would have been impossible to have time-consuming strong relationships with all these people.

| **BOX 20.1** | **Application of the HOW method of choice** |
|---|---|
| **H**esitate | In your first five seconds of contact with a 'stranger' (someone you have not met before) ask yourself, 'Do I want to form a weak relationship with this person?' If the answer is no, hesitate again and ask yourself, 'Why not?' |
| **O**utcome | What am I really seeking to achieve by forming a weak relationship with this person? Is it that over a period of time I can provide even more help and also that I can obtain more satisfaction from a wider circle of acquaintances? |
| **W**ay | W-thinking: Go out of your way to meet new people and strike up weak relationships with them. For example:<br>● Chat to someone you see in the elevator every day but have never chatted to before<br>● Walk around to another department and introduce yourself, explaining, 'I was just wondering what goes on round here?'<br>● Find out something interesting about each customer who rings up today<br>● Go and offer a chocolate cookie to the president's secretary |

- Obtain a list of company customers and call up three you have never spoken to before
- Sit next to someone new at lunchtime
- Participate in some 'out of hours' company activity you don't normally get involved in and find out about the people there W-thinking: The following are some 'relationship-initiating' microbehaviours you can choose from when encountering new people:
- Take an interest in each new person you meet
- Discover one interesting fact about each new person
- Find out the person's name and try to remember it (by associating with the interesting fact you have discovered)
- Pay this person a compliment (e.g. 'I really think that colour suits you')
- Make eye contact with each new person and smile warmly
- Ask an innocuous question, 'Is it still raining outside?' and then pursue the conversation
- Make a suggestion: 'Have you tried this?'
- Throughout the interaction reinforce everything you do (every behaviour, every word) with a positive emotion. For example 'encouragement' to continue the relationship , e.g. with statements, 'I am really pleased you came in'
- Demonstrate positive body language throughout the interaction
- End the interaction with an invitation, 'Please do come back and see us again'

**THE CHOICE CHALLENGE**

- Keep a list of 'acquaintances' (and their contact details) and expand the list by at least five people every week. The more you do so, the more you will love your work and people at work will love you.

# 21

# Choosing how to interpret values

## A key to management success is not just the values but the interpretation of the values

## The meaning of values

There is a substantial body of evidence which reveals that successful companies are those that are 'values driven'. However, it begs the question of what we mean by values and how to apply them in practice.

Many companies put too much emphasis on deciding and declaring their values and too little time helping people choose their practical interpretation of them.

The following are examples of some words that frequently pop up in the statements of 'core values':

- integrity
- innovative
- daring
- caring
- equality
- professional
- customer serving
- entrepreneurial
- a bias for action
- quality

There are, of course, hundreds of others from which companies choose. The trouble is that often few employees know what these fine words mean in practice. They are fine words but at the same time they are meaningless unless there is an effective interpretation of the behavioural choices available to apply them.

For example, integrity is as fine a core value as you can ever get. One could argue that integrity is essential in every aspect of business and management. But what the heck does it mean at 9.35 a.m. on a Tuesday morning when a supplier lets you down? Furthermore when a problem like this arises what do caring, daring or entrepreneurial even mean?

These words of course, can mean a lot but only if they are translated into specific behaviours. We thus have to choose our behavioural interpretations of these words. One of the ongoing challenges for managers is to help their teams interpret company values and apply them in their everyday behaviours. Such a challenge can present an excellent focus for team-building activities. 'Hi guys. We have this value called "being professional". Now can you all tell me what it meant in practice yesterday? Please choose some really good examples to illustrate what the word means.'

The key thing about values is that they are valuable. That means they are

**The key thing about values is that they are valuable.**

important, in fact so important that they need to be debated and addressed as frequently as possible. In this way teams can develop and choose their own interpretations of what the values mean in effective practice when any given situation arises.

Another key factor about values is that they are immutable. There is no going away from them without devaluing ourselves. Words like integrity, innovative and customer serving are so self-evident that hardly anyone can dispute them. Furthermore, they are hardly options from which to choose. Such values are virtually preordained and therefore are a given. The mistake that many companies make is that they think they can sit a group of people down in a conference room to choose their values. They cannot. Values are so intrinsic to our culture that they are there in the first place. We cannot cherry pick our values or, alternatively, have a menu of values presented to us from which to choose. Thus, if innovation is a value, it evolves from the way leaders followed by their employees choose to behave as a reflection of their own intrinsic personal beliefs. As soon as the value innovation is articulated it begs the question of interpretation: 'What does being innovative mean to us today?' It begs a *choice* of innovative behaviour.

The struggle in life and at work is not to choose our values but to bring them into focus, articulate them and then interpret what they mean in practice. We can play with related words (for example, creative, pioneering or initiating) and debate the semantic variations. However, ultimately the value is best reflected, not through the words, but through a macro- and microbehavioural interpretation (for example: we value innovation because it leads to something new or different which our customers, employees and company will prize – for example, the way customers no longer have to fill in forms as we do it for them).

| BOX 21.1 | Application of the HOW method of choice |
|---|---|

**H**esitate — Each day pluck out a core value and reflect on what it means in terms of your own macro- and microbehaviours
Furthermore, hesitate before you do something and ask yourself: 'In what way will this reflect the values that are important to me?'

**O**utcome — Identify the value that you are bestowing on a situation or on a person as a result of any behaviour of yours

**W**ay — W-thinking: Extend the range of macro- and microbehavioural options. Take a value (such as 'integrity') and try to brainstorm as many interpretations as possible as to what this means in practice at work. Then choose the best interpretation and apply it through your own behaviour (e.g. 'I will now ring back when I say I am going to ring back')

## THE CHOICE CHALLENGE

- Do something valuable today. Reflect your values onto another person.

# CHAPTER TWENTY-TWO

# Choosing to listen

## With so many people wishing to tell us things our most significant choices relate to those to whom we listen

### The listening choice

In the ideal world when two people meet each would do 50 per cent of the talking and each 50 per cent of the listening. Many people regrettably choose to do less of the latter and more of the former. They like the sound of their own voice – irrespective of whether the person opposite them is listening or not.

Choosing to listen to another person is not easy. It is hard work and consumes much more energy than talking. It requires immense powers of concentration as well as a heartfelt desire to understand other people. Furthermore, it requires a genuine interest in what others have to say. And that is where many managers fall down. They are not interested in others (excepting where it impinges on their own self-interest) and therefore not prepared to listen.

Thus when we choose to listen we are effectively choosing to hear about something that interests us and helps us – and perhaps learn more and understand better. The challenge any manager has is to choose what really interests him or her at work and can help him. If he is only interested in money (increasing profits by boosting revenues and reducing costs) then he will only choose to listen to people who can help him increase profits. If he is genuinely interested in the welfare of his employees then he will choose to listen to the stories of people's welfare so that he can help them more effectively.

There is a correlation, as yet unproven but supported by much circumstantial evidence, that those managers who choose to listen effectively are more successful than those who do all the talking. The managers who listen most develop their understanding of people at a far faster rate than those managers who think they know it all and therefore tell everybody all the answers.

When managers take an interest in people and choose to devote precious time to listening people feel valued. Most people like to have their views taken into account – even if they are not implemented. People like to have a hearing even if they do not always get what they want. Listening to one another strengthens social bonds. This is of critical importance in an organization where managers seek to bond people within the teams and communities they are working in.

Expressed another way, our listening choices will have a great impact on our future success. To use a simple analogy, when we turn on the radio we have a choice of over 30 stations to listen to. We can choose local radio, national radio, pop music, rap or rock, jazz, classical music, phone-in programmes, news programmes or serious talk shows. The simple choice we make about which radio station to listen to will have a major impact on our lives. Should we choose to listen only to classical music then the probability is that some of our future relationships will be conditioned on a mutual interest in classical music. Thus we will choose to listen to people who are interested in classical music. Contrariwise, if we choose to listen to a wide variety of music styles, sometimes jazz, sometimes rock and sometimes classical music then we effectively push back the boundaries of the circle of people with whom we can potentially form relationships.

The same principle applies to the people we meet at work. The more topics we choose to take an interest in the greater the number of people we will choose to listen to and therefore form effective relationships with. If we narrow our range of interest to one or two topics only we thus narrow the number of people we will listen to. This can be dangerous as we will alienate people who sense we are not interested in them.

Choosing to listen is therefore predicated on choosing what really interests us and choosing what we want to learn about, understand and who we want to help. The more we listen the more we will learn, understand and be able to help.

Choosing to listen is also more than mere information gathering or fact finding. The purpose of listening often extends to discovering the truth about a person or a given situation. Information and facts are impersonal and are relatively easily gleaned while the truth (together with wisdom) is personal and much more difficult to establish. It is through choosing to listen effectively – and using our curiosity and questioning ability – that we prise out the fundamental truths and wisdoms that are so essential for the conduct of our lives and the operation of our work.

**Through choosing to listen effectively we prise out the fundamental truths and wisdoms essential for the conduct of our lives and the operation of our work.**

There is an emotional dimension to listening. To ascertain the truth we have to assess, through the power of listening, not only the accuracy of each statement, not only the finesse with which the words are articulated, but also the degree and type of feeling with which each verbal expression is loaded. Words spoken with passion tell us one thing. The same words spoken in a monotone voice tell us another. When we choose to listen effectively we are not just listening to the words but also to the emotional undertones with which they are expressed. Angry words reveal a different truth to kind words. We have therefore to listen to the subtle nuances of the emotions and choose to measure the speaker's words accordingly.

| BOX 22.1 | Application of the HOW method of choice |
|---|---|
| **H**esitate | Always pause before speaking to another person. Try to be the first to listen |
| **O**utcome | Listen carefully so that the outcome of any conversation is enhanced learning and understanding as well as potential resolution of any issues arising. This will increase the probability of the necessary positive emotional or feel good outcomes |
| **W**ay | W-thinking: Extend the range of macro- and microbehaviours from which you can choose to facilitate and improve your |

effectiveness as a listener. For example, you might choose from the following:

- Make eye contact as the other person speaks (do not look away)
- Initiate facial expressions which indicate you are interested (or better still fascinated) in what the person is saying and that you understand
- Ask pertinent questions to deepen that understanding
- Replay (or repeat) some of the speaker's statements to reinforce the understanding
- Try to find points on which you agree and express those points
- Do not interrupt if you disagree with what is being said
- Hear the person out with minimal interruption
- Use warm body language and a friendly voice to encourage the person to continue speaking and open up – so that you can understand better
- Open your mind to the possibility that this person can influence you (rather than you influence them) i.e. be persuaded by them
- Only persuade the other person if you sense he wishes to be persuaded (in other words do not try to force a view on them)

## THE CHOICE CHALLENGE

- Jot down on a piece of paper how much time you spend listening to people today. The more you listen, the better you will be as a manager.
- Tomorrow jot down the outcomes of all the listening you did today (e.g. things you have learnt, actions that have been taken, behaviours that have changed, decisions that have been made, people who now feel better).

# 23

# Choosing maxims

## Challenge your own behaviours with your own choice maxims

## The need for maxims

Maxims are short-cuts to your philosophy of life. They are nuggets of wisdom, gleaned from experience, from study, from reading and learning from your mentors, which you choose to apply in your everyday life. Here are some examples of maxims from my own philosophy of life and work:

- Volunteer for every additional task that is going

- Always say 'yes', especially when others are saying 'no'

- Never be negative. If you feel negative then be positive. If you are tempted to say 'no' then try to find a way to say 'yes'

- Work harder than everyone else

- Say something at every meeting (but not everything)

- Mix with people you admire, but don't admire bad people

- Make yourself visible to important people

- Exude confidence. Never show doubt in front of important people (work out your doubts in private or in intimate settings with your closest confidants)

- Learn something new every day (and attend every training course going with the genuine aim of coming out of it a better person)

- Be curious. Ask questions. Take an interest in everybody and everything

- Listen intently, with the intent to understand, learn and help others

- For every ten words you speak listen to 40 words from others

- Never seek praise, but give it frequently and always with sincerity
- Show delight and enthusiasm as often as you can (but temper this with kindness and compassion when necessary)
- Change your mind every day
- Show people that you trust them and then they will rarely let you down (but it will happen)
- Be honest with yourself about your own weaknesses and then try to eliminate them (throw some light on your dark side)
- Create a work of art every day (if Martin Creed can win the 2001 Turner Prize for a light switching on and off then think what you can do with Blu-Tack or a crumpled ball of paper – although Martin Creed has done that too)
- Ensure the person you are with next is the most important person in the world
- Read something stimulating every day
- Inject emotion into your reasoning
- Always reflect on what you've done in order to identify a better way
- Set yourself the highest possible standards by observing the people with the highest standards – and copying them. Then go higher
- Never complain
- Before you can achieve you have to believe you can achieve
- Add up the numbers in ATTITUDE to create your target. Then go for ATTITUDE PLUS
- Face to face is better than the telephone. The telephone is better than letters or memos. These are better than e-mail. E-mail is better than nothing (only just)
- Excite the imaginations of your people, just like the best leaders do
- Radiate positive energy throughout your organization, just like the best leaders do
- Seize every interaction with a customer as an opportunity to do something special
- Use trust as the cornerstone in all your relationships. Trust is an emotion

- The people who win are the people who learn quickly. Learn fast

- Love your customers to death. If you love a customer the probability is the customer will love you

- Do at least one good deed every day

- In addition, make one gift every day to someone less well off than you

- Also make one gift every day to someone better off than you. (You do not need to tell the difference between less well off and better off. Merely make two gifts a day.)

- Make everyone you meet feel great

- Put your heart into everything you do (avoid getting into automatic mode – except when tying up your shoe laces)

- Never bear grudges about anyone. Get rid of them by looking for the good in everyone

- Do not use black ink or blue

- Show your love (in everything you do and for everyone you meet)

- There is always something in your life that can make you happy. Find it and show it. Every day!

- Take on challenges that are beyond you but not impossible. Then go beyond but do not be impossible

- Refuse any invitation to climb Mount Everest (and never throw snowballs with stones inside them)

- Never blame other people. For anything

- It is better to forgive and forget than remember the worst

- Reflect on at least one quotation of wisdom every day (e.g. Confucius said, 'The gold in one's heart is more precious than the gold in one's purse.'). These quotations are available in a thousand different places. Just go looking for them and you will find them. You can start here

- Talk to strangers. Be nice to everyone

- Make one new friend today and every day (when you get old you will never be lonely)

- Visit old people (or those that have retired or are ill or who are not currently in the mainstream of your work and life)

- Discover one fascinating new fact every day
- Celebrate someone else's achievements at least once a week
- Say and do nothing when provoked (never provoke or be provoked)
- Avoid being the same as everyone else. Make a difference (Be MAD)
- Wear a hat if you've never worn a hat before
- Keep the serious stuff until last then finish on a positive note
- Convince yourself something good will happen today. It will
- Laugh at least once a day but no more than ten times within any one hour
- Never finish a list with the number 58

There are, of course, tens of thousands more of these maxims. Ralph Waldo Emerson was an expert and so was Oscar Wilde. Confucius also excelled as did Lao Tzu. The Bible is full of them and so is the Buddhist *Dhammapada*. For example, the opening statement in the *Dhammapada* says: 'All that we are is the result of what we have thought.' Four paragraphs later it states 'For never does hatred cease by hatred. Hatred ceases by love; this is an eternal law.' Wow! What words of wisdom for any manager dealing with disaffected staff!

To make progress in your life and at work you need to choose your maxims carefully, absorb them into the various chambers of your soul, brain, heart and lungs, such that you can live them, think them, feel them and breathe them in making your everyday behavioural choices.

Study any successful person and you will discover that they always rely on a set of such maxims. For example Pavarotti once said: 'Others practice ten times to be good. I practice one hundred times to be good.' Allan Leighton, the ex Chief Executive of Walmart ASDA, said: 'Businesses don't die, people kill them. Furthermore businesses don't grow, people grow them.'

**Choose your maxims carefully, such that you can breathe them in making your everyday behavioural choices.**

Here is a suggestion. Photocopy sufficient copies of this section to send to your customers (better still buy them each a copy of this book!). Then invite your customers to select the ten maxims which are most appropriate to your relationship with them and e-mail them back to you. You might be surprised (as well as excited)!

---

**BOX 23.1**   **Application of the HOW method of choice**

**H**esitate — During your early morning ablutions select a maxim for the day

**O**utcome — Become a better person today by applying this maxim

**W**ay — W-thinking: Extend your range of maxims and then make a list of your favourite ones. Start with your top ten (you can write them on a postcard and send them to your friends – or at worst e-mail them)

Next invite each member of your team to compile their top ten. Use these to produce a list of your team's top 100 maxims. Have these statements designed onto a poster and call it your mission statement or core values. Everyone will be impressed

Select two maxims a week for the coming year to discuss with your team and apply.

Here are my two for this week:

- Read something stimulating every day (today it was Starbucks Christmas Survival Book – this made me laugh)
- Never blame other people. For anything. (My tongue hurts. I've bitten it so many times)

---

**THE CHOICE CHALLENGE**

- Choose your maxims wisely.
- If you have not chosen any maxims then you cannot be wise.

# CHAPTER TWENTY-FOUR

# Choosing memories

## How managers choose and use their memories is critical

### The use and misuse of memory

It is impossible to remember everything we learn. Most acquired knowledge sinks to the bottom of our subconscious and becomes hidden in the murky depths of our memory. In those dark interiors of our mind mental filing cabinets are non-existent and we thus struggle to trace ageing facts and figures. We fail to recall a name, a word let alone the basics of a foreign language we last spoke at school. Our memories become distorted with age, the good times of old becoming even better while the bad times are either blanked out or re-emerge as recurrent nightmares.

> **Most acquired knowledge sinks to the bottom of our subconscious and becomes hidden in the murky depths of our memory.**

It is on such foundations that many managers attempt to manage. As time passes by their in-depth knowledge and expertise darkens to protect the inner self from shining new lights.

The experienced manager is full of memories while the novice has no such depth from which to draw. It is these conflicting forces that generate the internal politics of many a company, where light faces dark, positive competes with negative and new practices vie with established principles.

The conflict is essentially between experience and new learning, between memory and the current lesson. Companies can be torn asunder when these vital forces oppose one another. Managers therefore need to choose their memories carefully and develop their experience accordingly.

They can choose memories which drive their prejudices and prove anything they like. Or they can choose memories which prove nothing except that everyone and everything is capable of change.

In choosing their memories managers can choose to take minutes, write reports, keep journals or create databanks. All provide memory support systems.

One senior vice-president I met prided himself on such a system. After he met an employee he would record the employee's name in a handheld computer (a PDA or personal digital assistant) together with one or two key facts about the employee. For example: 'BRISTOL SITE: Joe Smith, security guard, moustache, 19 years with company, loves playing darts. Twice married. Three grown-up kids. Current wife is Jill – has diabetes.'

Each time he visited the Bristol site he would tap into his handheld computer to remind himself of the people he was about to meet again. The employees loved him and he loved them. The cynics accused him of not being genuine, that he was using a device to maintain a pretence of being familiar with employees. His champions countered by saying the device was no different from a diary in which the birthdays of families and friends are recorded.

For a business to be built on relationships it is important that we make choices on what we remember about the people who form those relationships. If we choose to create bad memories then inevitably the relationship and the business will suffer. The challenge then is: 'What should we remember of a person? The good things or the bad things?' This choice of memory will influence our business through the behaviours we adopt as a result of the memory.

The challenge is to remember the good things about people. In doing so we ourselves will become good managers and our performance will be more effective for it. Employees will be motivated when you walk around and remind them of these good things. Reminiscence is part of the social bonding essential to any company and when this proves positive the outcome will invariably be positive too.

I have come across people who dwell on the negative, who drag from their memories all the things that have gone wrong over recent years and all the stories about the perpetrators of these wrongs. These people have chosen bad memories. They tell you of the strikes, of the terrible presentations someone gave, of the bad decisions that were made, of the way they were let down by various people. They do not tell you of the good things that happened. They have not chosen their memories wisely.

| **BOX 24.1** | **Application of the HOW method of choice** |
|---|---|
| **H**esitate | Spend a few moments at the end of every day reflecting on your positive memories of the day. Try to push the bad memories to one side |
| **O**utcome | Memories are the foundation for any future relationship. The outcome of any such relationship will therefore depend on your memory of it |
| **W**ay | W-thinking: Extend the range of memory options. View every situation and every person from as many different angles as possible and then choose the most positive memory. |
| | Discipline yourself to create a positive memory about every person you meet and every situation you are in. Even if there is a dreadful accident create a positive memory of the emergency crews who tackled the situation |

## THE CHOICE CHALLENGE

- Choose to have good memories. Your happiness will increase exponentially.

# CHAPTER TWENTY-FIVE

# Choosing to praise

## Praising is a lifestyle choice

### Praise as a heartset

Praise arises from a key heartset we choose for ourselves in relation to others. It is a very simple heartset. We choose to look for deeds and attributes we like in other people and then we choose to comment positively. That is praise.

Quite a few of us, driven by our subconscious, rarely make this choice. It does not occur to us as we go about our daily business that perhaps a word of praise would be welcomed by that person standing over there. We just take it for granted that people do things for us – unaware that our lack of acknowledgement of their efforts will gradually diminish what they do.

I have come across too many senior managers who have the attitude: 'I do not need to tell them they're doing a good job – they'll soon know when they're not.' In other words, in the absence of criticism you can assume you are doing all right.

Without exception every individual in every country I have visited has told me that they like to be praised, that they like to feel that their immense contribution to the company is valued and appreciated. However, most bosses choose not to do so or, if the company insists, they rely on an annual performance appraisal system to effectively 'systematize' praise. In the latter case praise becomes muted or distorted – especially if the performance appraisal is linked to a reward system in which only a minority of people can be praised for exceptional performance.

The level of praise in any one country is influenced by cultural dimensions. In one Asian country I know people are brought up not to praise each other. In this country if a child attains 97 per cent in school examinations then the parent will criticize, complaining: 'Why didn't you get 100%? You didn't work hard enough! Next time you will have to do better!' Yet most people in this Asian country love to be praised. It is just that they are deprived of it and therefore do not know how to do it.

The reverse is true in the USA where I find managers very liberal in their praise. They believe in transparency and therefore telling you how they feel. Thus if you do a great job they will praise you accordingly – and when you fall down they will also inform you. At least you know where you stand.

Praise is not a device to be offered like candy to solicit more performance from an employee. Praise must be genuine and must come from the heart. Whatever you are praising must genuinely make you feel good, genuinely delight or excite you. There must be a heartfelt emotional tag to any praising behaviour.

The opportunities to praise people are all around. The world is not so bad that there is nothing to praise within it. In fact, every day we can choose to seek out things to praise about other people. Praising is a lifestyle choice.

**The opportunities to praise people are all around.**

The benefits of praise are immeasurable. The more genuine praise you choose to give the greater the probability that what you praise will reoccur. Performance will be improved accordingly. Conversely, the more you choose to criticize the greater the probability that what you criticize will NOT reoccur – however, this does not mean that what you desire in its place will occur. As stated in an earlier chapter, criticism while frequently necessary must always be balanced with praise.

When you choose to give genuine praise from the heart people will warm to you, will value you – because you are honestly valuing them. It is a choice. The operative words here are genuine and balance; genuine because it must come from the heart and balance because too much of a good thing is bad for you. Too much praise is counterproductive (just like too much sugar is bad for you).

I was sitting in the Starbucks store at Millennia Walk, Singapore, drinking my caffe latte when one of the waitresses, Siska, passed by to clean a table nearby. She turned and said to me, 'I do like the tie you are wearing today.' I suddenly felt good. Siska is 20 years old. It occurred to me that she did not have to compliment me on my tie – in fact, I cannot recall another instance in the last 20 years when a waitress has praised anything about me. It was Siska's choice. As a manager you cannot write into the rule book or training manual, 'You must praise what customers are wearing.' All I know is that Edwin Seah, the store manager, frequently chooses to praise his team and the individuals in it. Furthermore, I also know that Michael Lee, who runs the Starbucks operation in Singapore, frequently chooses to praise Edwin Seah and the team – as well as all the other stores in Singapore.

**Every encounter with another human being is an opportunity to praise.**

Every encounter with another human being is an opportunity to praise. It seems so easy to criticize and spend more time doing this than praising. We are far better at complaining about poor service than choosing to write letters of praise when we receive good service. We are far better at reprimanding employees about substandard performance than choosing to praise them when they do a good job.

Praise must come from the heart and it must mean examining our own hearts to identify what makes us feel good about other people – and then choosing to do something about, for example, a word of praise here or a letter of compliment there.

Praise must never be routine, must never be applied mechanically as a result of a system. I have just downloaded my e-mail and, would you believe it, there is one entitled, 'You are a customer in a million.' For a moment, I think I might feel special, but then when I open the e-mail I realize it is just another piece of spam trying to seduce me into a purchase. For them I am not a customer in a million, in the sense of being special – in fact I am just number 735,661 in a million. I do not exist in this company's mind or heart, only in its computer. The statement is meaningless if not hypocritical. It lacks integrity.

| BOX 25.1 | Application of the HOW method of choice |
| --- | --- |

**H**esitate     In every encounter you have with every single person hesitate and ask yourself: 'In what way can I praise this person?'

**O**utcome     Genuine praise always makes people feel good. But it has to be genuine (and thus come from the depths of your heart)

**W**ay     W-thinking: Extend the range of praising options

Try to extend your praise to as many people you meet as possible. Here are some examples you can choose from:

- To the security guard: 'You always look so smart in that uniform'
- To the stranger in the lift: 'That's a really nice perfume you are wearing. Can you tell me what it is?'
- To the systems engineer: 'I'm really impressed with your knowledge of this system'
- To a customer: 'Let me be honest with you. I welcome your complaint. I really do appreciate the effort you made to ring in and tell me about the problem'
- To your boss: 'I appreciate the time you have given me – and I mean that. You are always available for me'
- To your company president (a letter or e-mail): 'The initiative you took in organizing the company barbecue for all employees was really well received. I enjoyed it immensely. It was great fun'
- To the production assistant: 'I can always rely on you on getting things done. Unlike others you've never ever let me down'
- To the sales consultant: 'Can I just tell you that when we were out on the road the other day I was incredibly impressed by your approach. You seem to have an excellent rapport with all your customers. I'm convinced this accounts for your first-class results'
- To the customer service agent in the call centre: 'You are always so cheerful and happy. Congratulations – it's so refreshing to speak with you'

- To the graduate trainee: 'I like your new hairstyle. It's very avant-garde. I think I'll get one myself'

---

**THE CHOICE CHALLENGE**

- Keep a 'praise diary' and every day jot down at least three different occurrences when you have praised people.

# CHAPTER TWENTY-SIX

# Choosing rationalities

## Reason is relative, not absolute

### The emotional nature of reason

If you think you are rational then you are being irrational. The rationalities we use at work and in everyday life are a product of emotional choices and will vary according to what we feel, believe and value. There is a wide range of rationalities we can choose from in arriving at any decision. That is why politicians disagree so much and many others too.

**If you think you are rational then you are being irrational.**

Everyone has a reason for doing something. It is just that other people have different sets of reasons for doing things differently. For example, in the mid-19th century the vast bison herds that roamed the Great Plains of North America virtually disappeared as a result of hunting. The American hunters had their reasons. However, the preservationists who founded the Yellowstone National Park in 1872 had a totally different reason: to protect the few remaining animals.

Everything we do has a reason, but often those reasons differ from those of other people. The cause of all wars, conflict and violence is differing reasoning processes or (if you are drunk or drugged) distorted reasoning processes. In other words, conflict is a result of conflicting reasoning processes. To avoid the bloodshed and antagonism that conflict frequently brings civilized societies have managed to create a social system in which differences in reasoning are channelled through a process of democracy. With few exceptions democracy is not a process well known in most commercial (or even public) organizations where dictatorial leadership still prevails. Dictators choose their reasons and others have to accept them. Otherwise you are out.

Social groups tend to form when people choose to share the same reasoning processes. Harmony results from this shared reasoning processes and leads to the declaration: 'We all feel the same way on this issue.' In commercial companies a major contributor to long-term success will be this shared reasoning process (as opposed to a dictated reasoning process – as evident in company edicts). Companies are often brought down by people choosing different sets or rationales relating to the business. These disagreements are manifested by strikes, senior management disputes, disaffection of customers and alienation of shareholders.

As stated earlier the main driving force behind our reasoning processes, or rationales, is the binary code of emotions. We move towards what makes us feel good and move away from what makes us feel bad. There is thus no absolute about rationality because we all feel differently about different situations. To create the harmony necessary for sustained success in business we therefore have to choose our rationalities carefully as well as open our minds to the possibilities that other rationalities might be preferable in guiding our behaviour to a desired outcome.

As we have already seen, we make choices on how we see people, on the assumptions we use and on what we value. Combined together these perceptions, assumptions and values are key factors in the way we choose our rationality.

A common rationality is to buy the cheapest. However, there might be good arguments for buying exactly the same item at a slightly higher price. Quality of after-sales service is just one factor that might affect the choice.

Many of us make different choices on the rationales on how to handle people. For example, one rationale is to fire a poor performer if he fails to improve after two warnings. Others might argue that a warning of poor performance becomes a self-fulfilling prophecy and therefore a better way is to coach, counsel and encourage over an extended period of time to help an individual realize his full potential.

These choices relating to rationales face us every day and are particularly pertinent if we are managers. We have to make choices such as:

- Do we see people as costs (rationale 1)?

● Do we see them as assets (rationale 2)?

Despite what many managers think we cannot choose both of these rationales.

Choosing to see people as costs (rationale 1) means seeing employees as disposable commodities. We hire them when times are good and fire them when times are bad. Furthermore, we pay them the least we can get away with. Conversely, rationale 2 leads us to investing in people, holding on to them as long as we can and motivating them by demonstrating that we value them. So we pay the best in the marketplace – rather than the least. Not every company pays the same for the same job – thus revealing different rationalities relating to motivation.

Thus as managers we have to choose our rationales and these choices will drive our behaviours and have a critical impact on an outcome such as the motivation of employees.

Some further examples of choices available to us in terms of rationales can be found in Box 26.1.

| BOX 26.1 | Rationales |
|---|---|

| | |
|---|---|
| **Choice 1** | I did not ring her **because** I was so busy (i.e. she was low on my priority list at that moment) |
| **Choice 2** | I rang **because** I wanted to get back to her as quickly as possible (i.e. she was important to me) |
| **Choice A** | I did not offer him the job **because** he lacked the requisite experience; this is despite his obvious potential and passion for the work |
| **Choice B** | I have offered him the job **because** he has so much potential and passion for this work, despite his lack of experience |
| **Choice X** | I cannot authorize your attending this conference in Asia **because** I am not convinced it is necessary, especially given our tight budget situation |
| **Choice Y** | I would be delighted for you to attend this conference in Asia **because** I believe it would bring you and the company so much benefit and would thus be a worthwhile investment |

## BOX 26.2 Application of the HOW method of choice

**H**esitate    Ask yourself, 'What is the rationale behind the decision I am about to make or behind my next behaviour?'

**O**utcome    Where does this reasoning lead to? What will be the result if I behave this way (or make this decision) using this rationale?

**W**ay    W-thinking: Extend the range of rationales from which to choose and then examine the possibility of choosing a different way based on a different rationale. For example:

- Is there a probability of a better 'feel good' outcome if I choose to listen to another person's rationale, accept it and apply it?

- Why am I disagreeing with this person? Why not find elements of his argument I can agree with and apply (e.g. say 'Yes' to this rather than 'No' to that)

- Use the classic approach of 'putting yourself in the other people's shoes' to understand how they feel (e.g. in the face of a complaint do not become defensive – using your own rationale – but become understanding – accepting their rationale)

- Take a risk with a different rationale to the one you normally use (e.g. 'I'll take my time over this' rather than 'I need to rush')

- Challenge your first inclination and find a reason for doing the opposite, then do the opposite (e.g. 'I'm going to hold back on this information' vs 'I'll willingly make this information widely available')

- Create positive rationales and try to discard negative ones (e.g. 'I will see this person' instead of 'I won't see this person')

- Find ways of working WITH people who think differently from you as opposed to working AGAINST them

- Be reasonable. Try to choose an even better reason than the one you are holding now. It will make you and others feel better.

# Choosing responses

## Our choice of responses to any situation influences our successes and failures in life

### A thousand different responses from which to choose

A friend in Singapore, Ann Tay, has just sent me an e-mail which states:

**"10% of life is made up of what happens to you. 90% of life is decided by how you react"**

The e-mail then goes to provide many examples of this principle. We might argue forever whether the percentages are correct. More important is the principle. Every day we experience external events, some expected and some unexpected, some minor and some major (for example, September 11 2001). It is our choice of response to these which influences our successes and failures in life. Whatever the event we invariably have many more options from which to choose than we think.

For example, if our boss shouts at us our range of choices in how to respond is very wide. For example, we can:

- hit him in the face
- swear at him
- go and complain to his boss
- poke our tongue out at him
- make a joke
- smile and nod

- shout back at him
- resign there and then
- automatically go on the defensive
- invite him to calm down
- invite him for a coffee
- put our arms around him and hug him
- invite him to explain
- praise him for his perception
- throw water at him
- whistle politely while he rants on
- tap our fingers on the desk
- make a note of everything he says
- call for a witness and ask him to repeat the allegations
- threaten to take him to court for bullying and harrassment
- give him a 'V'- sign
- give him a thumbs up
- give him a thumbs down
- laugh at him
- ignore him
- walk away
- look out the window and sigh
- agree with everything he says
- disagree with everything he says
- listen and try to learn something

There are, of course, many more options. And I suspect that most of us would not even consider most of these. We would respond automatically in the same way we have always done when someone shouts at us.

When a customer complains how do we respond? Again there are thousands of different options from which to choose. When an employee is not performing too well how do we respond? Once more there are thousands of options.

Most companies try to regulate (and therefore restrict) their people by prescribing responses through policy and procedure. 'This is what you should do if this happens.' However, this is very limited and frequently ineffective for the simple reason that it is impossible to predict every eventuality and further it is undesirable to treat employees like robots, programmed to respond in a specified way.

For example, when a team member comes in late for the third time in four days how should we respond? The options are countless and the rulebooks are of little use in these situations. The same applies when an employee goes sick, we win an important order, the figures decline, the figures improve, there is a major organizational change, our competitors come out with a superior product, our customers defect, our employees give us some painful feedback and so on with most things that happen at work. Do we turn a blind eye when we see something we shouldn't?

Rulebooks cannot cope with these types of behavioural issues that confront managers every day of their working lives. Yet they are behavioural issues which have a critical impact on performance. These issues therefore have to be addressed with an effective choice of responses.

For example, if a team member tells us that she is fed up doing the same old thing day in and day out we have to choose our response. The same applies when a new member of the team announces she is pregnant or when we hear gossip that one of our star performers is having an affair with our own boss or when a customer starts shouting at us down the phone. Another situation might be when our boss criticizes us, unfairly in our opinion. In each case (and the thousands of others) we have to choose our response. Most of our life we spend choosing responses and on most occasions we give little thought to these responses. We act instinctively or as we have always done.

In all probability the 10:90 'rule' stated earlier is correct; most of our macro- and microbehaviours reflect our choice of response to external events, to what is happening in this world, to what happens at home and at work and to what other people say. Inappropriate responses to these stimuli just make things worse. Thus an unkind word from someone we do not like can provoke an unwarranted response on our part. This in turn provokes a further response and a chain of events that has the potential to cause great damage to a valued relationship. People are always falling out over their responses to each other.

**People are always falling out over their responses to each other.**

The reason that most times we do not think about these responses is because they are frequently automatic and driven by subconscious processes that have developed over a lifetime of learning and experience.

This 'automated response process' is reinforced (and sometimes exacerbated) by the many training programmes that are designed to develop automatic responses. This might well be appropriate for airline pilots training in the simulator and learning how to respond to an engine failure. It might also be appropriate for local authorities preparing contingency plans for flooding. It is definitely appropriate for fire and rescue authorities reacting to emergency calls. However, it is inappropriate in relationships. As indicated in an earlier book[1] as soon as we get into preprogrammed automatic responses in any relationship we put that relationship at risk. We get into routines and habits which will drain the emotional energy from a relationship. As a result our responses to our spouses, children and colleagues at work become automatic. It is the automatic frown, the automatic gesture of defiance, the arms crossing, the sigh, the look out of the window and the intimidating stare.

It is the same with the words we choose in responding to people. For example the way we say 'thank you' is frequently the same; it becomes an automatic virtually unthinking response. Similarly, when we are criticized many of us go into automatic mode in defending ourselves. We say: 'You don't understand ...' or 'I don't think you are being fair ...' It is always the same response; most of us are that predictable. In fact, many managers spend much of their time anticipating and speculating on people's responses. 'If we present the problem this way this will happen, while if we present it that way that will happen.'

We gamble on people's responses and frequently lose out. Managers who are the winners are those who carefully consider their own choice of responses. That way they learn. Automatic responses in relationships are incredibly dangerous while well-considered chosen responses frequently prove fruitful.

| **BOX 27.1** | **Application of the HOW method of choice** |
| --- | --- |

**H**esitate     Pause for a few seconds before making any response to another person

**O**utcome     Ask youself what the ideal outcome should be of this response in terms of making the other person and yourself feel good

**W**ay     W-thinking: Extend the range of potential macro- and microbehavioural responses. Use the examples just given to practise with. For a second practice run try this one. When it comes to team achievements what responses do you choose? Do you:

- look out for these achievements in the first place?
- ignore achievements?
- pat people on the back when they achieve things?
- send them personalized cards?
- send them hand-written letters?
- pull the team together for an impromptu celebration?
- call up your own boss to extol the virtues of the achievers?
- go round asking them what they've achieved today, this week, this month?
- award stars, stickers or vouchers
- put their names up in lights
- post their names on a 'well done' notice board
- clock up 'brownie points' for them using some form of points accumulation system
- start your team meetings focusing on who has achieved what
- invent different types of rewards (e.g. 'take Friday afternoon off', 'have a meal with your family at your local Chinese restaurant and send me the bill to pay' etc.)
- etc. etc. etc. (a thousand etceteras)

- For every external eventuality (whatever happens to you) create an extended range of responses from which to choose, and then choose wisely.

## Note
**1** *The Stimulus Factor* by David Freemantle, FT Prentice Hall, 2001

# CHAPTER TWENTY-EIGHT

# Choosing what to see in a person

## We see what we choose to see

### Choosing to see people in a different way

You have never seen a real person in your life! That's the truth. What you see in another person is what you choose to see – and often what you choose to see is nothing and therefore you do not see the person. You walk right on by and you ignore somebody. You even neglect to say 'hello'.

**You have never seen a real person in your life!**

The young woman looks for a hero in a future husband and therefore is impressed by the heroic nature of her newly found boyfriend. Years later after marriage she attains a greater sense of reality. He is not a hero after all – the heroic strands in his nature were only 5 per cent of his make-up, but that is all she saw. She did not see the remaining 95 per cent. Perceptions change as we get to know people. Often to know them better we have to challenge those perceptions and choose better ones.

We see what we choose to see and this is at the root of all prejudice. Jew, Arab, American, Asian, Gipsy, Jehovah's Witness, black man, white man, terrorist, freedom fighter, gay, lesbian, politician, trade unionist, tramp or rich man – we choose our image based on limited experiences, often third hand, and then select the tiny bits of current reality that conform to our previously chosen images – thus reinforcing our prejudice.

I have listened to thousands of people in hundreds of organizations tell me that their bosses do not see it their way. And then I chat with the bosses who tell me the opposite – their employees do not see it their way.

It is just that we all choose to see things differently – and see people differently too.

To make things different (or to make a difference) we have to choose to see things in a different way. We behave differently when we see things differently. One person will see a customer who is angry and act defensively while another will see the self-same customer as in need of help – and therefore behave with compassion and understanding in trying to resolve the problem.

If we choose to see our employees in a bad light then it is virtually guaranteed that all we will notice is their bad behaviour. If we see them as 'nine-to-fivers' who are not committed, who shirk behind our backs and produce shoddy work then that is what we will get. Conversely, if we choose to see our teams as dedicated, hard working and passionate then this is also what we will get. What we see is what we get.

Therefore, to get more we have to *see* more in the first place. We have to choose the half-full jug rather than the half-empty one. We have to choose to see the good in a person rather than the bad – and we are all good and bad to a greater or lesser degree (depending, of course, on how we see it).

There are stories circulating in most companies of people who have made good after others have rejected them. For example, the troublemaker who was rejected by the old regime for being too outspoken, too negative and a destabilizing influence suddenly becomes a star in the new regime. His talent for pushing back the boundaries, for questioning traditional thinking, for being creative is suddenly harnessed to great effect. The storybooks are full of such heroes and heroines, whether they be Martin Luther, Jeanne d'Arc, Beethoven, the Beatles or Andy Warhol.

If we want to change people the first thing we have to do is change the way we see them. In this way, we will change our behaviour and hopefully they will respond accordingly. If we see a colleague in an unfavourable light then our own behaviour will be conditioned by this and in all probability our colleague will respond accordingly, reinforcing the view. We therefore need to choose to see our colleagues in a favourable light. In doing so we will start generating positive behaviours and they will echo this in due course.

It is all too easy too dismiss other people because of the bad light we choose to see them in. We need to change the light, to choose rosier tints in our view finders. This means improving our perceptions of people. There is hardly a single person in the world who would want to be viewed in a bad light – thus if we can throw the good light on people we will begin to see them differently.

Our performance as managers is thus conditional on the way we see people. To improve our performance we need to choose to see people in the best possible light. We should choose to see each customer as a phenomenal asset as opposed to a bloody nuisance, we should choose to see each employee as a hard-working person who is genuinely doing their best as opposed to some-one who is trying to rip off the company with a minimal work effort.

Ultimately, the way we choose to see other people reflects the way we choose to see ourselves. If we see ourselves as being full of love for the greater body of humanity then this will be reflected in our relationships with most people we meet. Conversely, if we see ourselves as the victims of people fighting against us then we will restrict our relationships within highly protective boundaries that preclude many.

When a child enters a candy shop all he sees are the candies. He does not see the shopkeeper. Similarly there is an old Indian saying: 'When a pick-pocket meets a saint all he sees are the pockets.'

This has particular relevance in management. Thus when people see a fierce-looking senior executive coming all they see is potential criticism – and so they act accordingly providing a cursory smile as he passes by and telling him what he wants to hear should he ask a question. Senior executives rarely see reality. They choose what they want to see – and then see it. If they want to see motivated people they will see them – and woe betide any harbinger of bad news who tells them people are demotivated.

This disability of seeing exactly what we want to see applies equally to ourselves. If we see ourselves as being the expert, as the person who knows best then we will naturally see the faults in others who do not conform to our own high standards. Conversely, if we choose to see ourselves as humble human beings then we will see other people as experts – and all our behaviours and relationships will change accordingly.

Thus in choosing the way we see people we have to choose the way we see ourselves. Furthermore, we have to be so brutally honest with ourselves that we see ourselves for what we are. When we fail to do this there is a negative impact on others as we act out a role divorced from the reality of our true self.

Too many people have a highly sanitized perception of themselves. They are well able to see the spots on other people's faces but are totally unable to see the spots on their own. They deny what they see of themselves because they do not like what they see. To make progress in life and at work it is essential that we face up to these unpalatable truths about ourselves. In this way we become true both to ourselves and to others.

| BOX 28.1 | Application of the HOW method of choice |
|---|---|
| **H**esitate | Spend a moment thinking, 'How do I see this person?' |
| **O**utcome | Following on from the previous challenge ask yourself: 'What am I looking for in this person? Can I see this person in a different light – even a more positive light?' |
| **W**ay | W-thinking: Imagine each person you encounter, whether that person be a stranger or someone you know, as a multi-faceted diamond: |

- Try to view this person from as many different facets as possible
- Try to identify the good positive facets - i.e. to see this person in a good light
- Having changed the light in which you see a person allow this to be reflected in your behaviour. Here are examples of microbehavioural options from which you can choose:
  - take more interest in this person
  - make this person feel special
  - listen more effectively to this person
  - compliment this person more frequently
  - confide in this person more
  - give this person more time
  - avoid avoiding this person
  - trust this person more

–  enjoy more of this person's company

## THE CHOICE CHALLENGE

- Look at your boss, members of your team – and even yourself – and choose to see each in a different light.

# Choosing stimuli

## To succeed managers must stimulate their thinking with new ways

### The stimulus factor

Routine can be like a drug, reducing managers and their teams to mind-numbing soporific states as they fall into subconscious automatic mode and process whatever they have forever been processing.

Some people like this; it anaesthetizes them from the rudeness of the real world. Routine can be an escape from mental agonies, broken hearts and physical distress. Routine can substitute boredom for the pain of everyday life. Furthermore, routine conserves energy – when in routine mode we no longer have to think for ourselves or work out what work we need to do. We just follow the numbers and become a number too.

> **Routine can be an escape from mental agonies, broken hearts and physical distress.**

When we get into routine we merely go through the motions using preset programmes and procedures. We are effectively robots. We do not need minds and definitely not hearts. We just 'tick over nicely'.

In the dark ages before computers were invented routines were the only things most of us had to work on. Every day was the same. The task was repetitive. A thousand times we would fill in the form, add up the figures and complete the operation. We would think nothing of it – because there was nothing to think about. That was work! For most of us it was a thought-less activity that took us through 40 hours of energetic necessity to produce a slice of bread for the family and a roof over their heads.

Now we have computers that can perform all the routines for us. So we need to think for ourselves if we are to earn a living. This is tough for people not used to expending emotional and intellectual energy.

Customer service routines are best left to computers and equipment. However, the all-important customer and employee relations on which successful businesses are built cannot be left to routine. They require the stimulus of variation.

To succeed, managers must choose to stimulate their thinking with new ways and further stimulate their teams with new ways of motivation. As explained in a previous book, *The Stimulus Factor*, there are thousands of different stimuli a manager can choose to stimulate the motivation of his or her people. For example, a manager can set a daily challenge as a stimulus or he can stimulate people with new learning or new forms of reward. The opportunities are endless. Here are three:

- When initiating a conversation (with a team member or a customer) choose to stimulate the relationship with a different opening gambit. In other words do not open up with the same 'How are you?' type question each time

- When making a proposal to your boss try a different stimulus. Do not use the same format, the same old words – but try a different approach to stimulate his or her interest

- When preparing a presentation do not use the standard six bullet points and familiar backdrops. Create a personal and unique work of art which will stimulate your audience

The challenge is to choose a fresh set of stimuli every day.

However, a word in defence of routines. As previously stated they are essential when it comes to operating mechanical equipment. I am not suggesting for one moment that the airline pilot jettison his routine for getting the plane into the air, neither am I suggesting that you ditch your routine for fastening your seatbelt in the car. Routines can be incredibly useful. However, they are useless in the field of personal relationships and can actually precipitate the erosion which causes relationships to end.

The challenge is to go beyond the routine and choose to stimulate the relationship you have with others – by doing something different.

Successful managers are always looking for new ideas to stimulate the motivation of their teams. To this extent they choose to stimulate themselves by taking an interest in their team, reading books, attending fascinating training seminars and meeting stimulating people.

One manager I know chooses to play music to his team. They have their own theme tunes and these vary from time to time. Another manager I know occasionally chooses to start his team meetings by going round the room inviting each person to say something positive about another person present. They keep going until everyone has had something positive said about them.

A third manager I know chooses to stimulate his team by holding meetings in different venues. Sometimes they go to Starbucks for a coffee, other times they stroll to the park where they sit on the grass, other times they take a trip on a riverboat. The possibilities are endless if only you choose to create them and seize them.

Every day there are opportunities to search out some valuable resource to stimulate you. Personally I like quotes. I collect quotes. I pull them out of newspapers, magazine articles and also scribble in the margin of books. I then use these quotes to stimulate my own thought processes. For example, I love the quote from the Bible: 'For where your treasure is there your heart will be also' (Matthew 6:21).

I watch films and obtain an immense number of positive stimuli from these. For example, go and see *Buena Vista Social Club* for the ultimate stimulus. It is not a management film but it will teach you a lot about creativity and the motivation of people.

| **BOX 29.1** | **Application of the HOW method of choice** |
|---|---|
| **H**esitate | Before doing anything consider the possibility of doing it differently to make it more stimulating |
| **O**utcome | The use of different stimuli enables a relationship to remain fresh and energized as opposed to tired and jaded |

**W**ay

W-thinking: Extend the range of stimuli you use in everyday life and at work. Here are some stimulating choices:

- Use art (music, pictures etc.) to stimulate your team
- Do something different at lunchtime
- Do something different with your team at 3.00 p.m. each afternoon (for example two minutes' meditation)
- Discuss a 'quote of the day'
- Discuss a 'word of the day'
- Highlight an achievement/success every hour/day/week
- Wear something different on the last Friday of every month
- Have monthly surprises (keep them under wraps for 29 days)
- Have one day a month free of internal e-mails
- Use postcards instead of e-mails

## THE CHOICE CHALLENGE

- Choose to become an incredibly stimulating person.

# CHAPTER THIRTY

# Choosing your walls

## You can tell an organization by its internal walls

### Wall-to-wall choosing

Whatever is put on the walls reflects the ethos of the organization. Believe it or not someone chooses what goes on the walls.

One insurance company I visited had nothing on its walls. The company had a nice modern building with gleaming smokey glass windows on its external façade. But everything inside was grey. My first meeting was in a conference room with some senior executives. The walls were grey and there was nothing on them – not one single picture. Later I walked round the offices of this company including its call centre which was housed in this building. Everyone had their eyes down. They looked bored. The corridors near the elevators had no pictures. The whole place was characterless and so were the majority of its people. This reflected the rather uninspired communications they had with their customers. Everything was matter of fact. There were just two dimensions in everything they did and it was black and white with shades of grey in between. The whole organization lacked colour – and so did its people.

**Whatever is put on the walls reflects the ethos of the organization.**

One or two brave people had tried to stick photos of their families and friends on the walls but had been reprimanded by the building services department which had accused them of damaging the walls. This might come as a surprise to any of you who have walls at home, but sticking or hanging things on walls actually damages them! What a dreadful thought! It is a thought they chose to have in this rather mundane, uninspired and most boring insurance company.

A public service organization I visited in the north of England did have things on its walls, but these were rules and regulations. Hanging in most corridors were large display boards full of closely typed memos detailing what staff should and (mostly) should not do with respect to health and safety, fire procedures, first aid, bomb alerts, bank holidays. This was coupled with information on bus timetables, organization changes, new appointments and productivity targets and measures. I never saw anyone studying these noticeboards. Nobody paid any notice to the noticeboards! They were a real turn-off.

However, in some companies I have seen walls I like; walls with interesting pictures bought in art galleries, walls where staff have created a lot of visual interest, walls with balloons and streamers hanging on them, walls celebrating the frequent successes of the team, walls setting some fantastic awe-inspiring challenges for the people that week, walls with jokes, walls with quotes, walls with cartoons and walls which stimulate an immense amount of visual interest.

Visit Puccino's restaurant in the Royal Station Arcade in Windsor in the UK to see some really inspired internal walls. I have stared at them many times and I still laugh. (For example, the following notices are scrawled on the white walls in black: 'Our camel beer is rubbish, don't drink it!!!' Or: 'Don't worry, we have plenty of sugar sachets. And we have toilets too.')

Another example is the ASDA store at Chippenham near Slough in the UK. A back office noticeboard is headed 'Colleague Involvement' and refers to such important subjects as, 'Suggestions and ideas,' 'Rewarding colleagues,' 'Celebration buffets,' 'Champion roles,' 'Colleague circles' and 'We're listening surveys'.

The back office of the Holiday Inn in Leicester in the UK also has some inspirational pictures on its noticeboards, with photographs of employees with pertinent and inspirational quotes coming out of their mouths. Kevin Burley, the General Manager of this hotel, was so impressed with one of his frontline staff, who was an amateur painter, that he invited him to paint murals on the walls leading to the leisure centre.

A few years back the call centre at Hyder Utilities in St Mellons, Cardiff in Wales, had a noticeboard on each side of the entrance. One was a 'smiley' noticeboard and the other a 'sad' one. If Jack came to work looking sad then his colleagues would put a yellow Post-it note on the 'sad' noticeboard stating, 'Jack looks sad today'. Conversely, if Jill came to work looking happy then her colleagues would post a note on the 'smiley' noticeboard saying so. There are endless variations on this theme. For example, another company I know has a well done noticeboard on the wall. Any person or team seen to be doing something exceptional is given an accolade through having a 'well done' notice posted on the board. Any employee or manager can award such an accolade.

None of this happens by default. What goes on the internal walls of any organization is a result of choices made by certain individuals. The executive choices are therefore twofold:

● What types of wall do we want?

● Who chooses what should go on these walls?

The overall principle of choice should be that whoever has to sit and stare at the walls should from time to time choose what goes on these walls. Thus the team of receptionists should be involved in what goes on the walls in reception and the call centre team should choose what goes on their walls. If you have your own office then obviously you should choose what goes on your wall.

| BOX 30.1 | Application of the HOW method of choice |
|---|---|

**H**esitate    As you walk through your offices tomorrow morning pause for a while and look at the walls from a fresh perspective. How do they grab you?

**O**utcome    What is the environment we should be seeking to reflect through our walls?

**W**ay    W-thinking: Extend the range of options. Brainstorm out as many options as possible for adorning the walls of your office environment. The following is a list of options for adorning the walls at your place of work

     ● Pictures/photos from an art gallery

     ● Pictures/photos from teammates

- Pictures/photos from the local community (e.g. kids from the local school)
- Mirrors
- Murals (painted by experts)
- Murals (painted by amateurs)
- Famous quotes (serious)
- Famous quips (funny)
- Cartoons
- Competitions (e.g. employee of the month)
- Reports of interest to passers-by
- Reports of no interest to passers-by
- Surveys ('let us know what you think')
- Space for 'Post-it' note ideas
- Balloons, streamers and physical decorations
- Exhortations (e.g. 'reach this target this week and you will be well rewarded)
- Praise boards (or well done noticeboards)
- Happy/sad boards (who looks happy, who looks sad)
- Rules and regulations
- Company announcements

## THE CHOICE CHALLENGE

- Carry out the following exercise:

| This is what is on our walls | This is the corporate ethos our walls reflect |
| --- | --- |
| ............................................... | ............................................... |
| ............................................... | ............................................... |
| ............................................... | ............................................... |
| ............................................... | |

# 31

# Choosing who to talk to

## We need to extend the circle of people we choose to talk to

## Talking to strangers

Yesterday was Sunday. It was a beautiful day and I was on the waterfront with my daughter Ruth-Elena at Mayflower Park,[1] Southampton, in the UK. We noticed a man about to pass us on a bicycle. He was riding it casually in a wobbly sort of way. He was dressed in jeans and looked a little unkempt. Taking his hands off the handlebars he waved to me and shouted, 'Good morning sir!' and then cycled on. I waved back and shouted, 'Good morning.' Ruth-Elena commented: 'I think that man is a bit loopy.'

This morning the same type of thing happened. I was walking from my home into Windsor town centre for a business meeting at Puccino's (I tend to hold many of my business meetings in cafés). As I strolled along enjoying the sun I sensed someone striding up behind me. I glanced over my shoulder and saw a rather dishevelled man with a lanky gait, walking briskly with accentuated movements of his arms and legs, almost like a soldier marching. 'It's a beautiful day isn't it?', he said to me as he passed me by. 'It makes you happy to be alive!' I echoed his sentiment and conversed with him briefly before he strode on. Instinctively, I was relieved he had passed on and not hung back to engage me in further conversation. I noticed that he spoke to everyone in the street. He even tapped on the window of the hairdressers to give the people inside a thumbs-up sign. I thought he was mad.

And then I thought that perhaps I'm mad. Why do I and my daughter react when complete strangers, albeit behaving a little unusually, pass by and say

'Good morning'? Is it mad to greet complete strangers with a passing comment? Is it mad to assume the worst because strangers are behaving differently from how I would?

Most of us choose not to speak to the strangers who pass us by. We choose not to speak to the people in the elevator or the people we sit next to on the bus, the train or the plane. Most times we choose not to speak to the people sitting opposite us in a restaurant or to the people standing in line with us in a queue. We choose not to speak to people we do not know. This is totally irrational. Or it could be totally rational. (We use deep-rooted emotions to choose our reasons and rationalities. There is no absolute when it comes to rationality: what is rational to one person is irrational to another.)

**We choose not to speak to people we do not know. This is totally irrational. Or it could be totally rational.**

To extend our influence as managers we therefore need to extend the range of people we talk to and from time to time include those people we do not know. The people we tend to talk to are those within our comfort zones and at work these include our colleagues, our bosses and team members plus people we know in other departments. We only talk to people we do not know when they are introduced to us by others or when there is some pretext that links us to the unknown person.

We also tend to talk to people we like and avoid talking to people we dislike. We choose to avoid certain people. Again we limit our range. The key is to find things we like in other people; then we can start talking to them.

Watch people entering a conference room and see who they talk to. Most times it is people they know. Rarely do they introduce themselves to people they do not know. Watch managers walking through a large open-plan office and see who they talk to. It will be people they know. Rarely do they start chatting to people they do not know.

We feel comfortable and secure talking to people we know (because we have knowledge of them) while we subconsciously fear talking to people we do not know (because we have no knowledge of them). We thus limit ourselves subconsciously. We limit the opportunities to build new relationships and we limit the opportunities to learn from new people. We limit ourselves because of the fear of the unknown.

However, no manager can be successful if he (or she) fears the unknown. The challenge therefore is to choose to talk to more strangers, especially at work. In this way we extend our circle of acquaintances (see Chapter 20 on 'initiating relationships').

If we want to be totally rational about these choices then we should talk to every single person who passes us by. Just as the man on the bicycle did yesterday or just as the man striding past me this morning did. But I thought they were both mad! In fact, it is I whom am probably being mad (irrational) – I accept that on very rare occasions if we talk to strangers we might get attacked, but on the large majority of occasions this does not happen. Admittedly, it is a risk but it is a very small one. Using just a little bit of common sense (do not talk to strangers in dark back alleys after midnight) we minimize that risk. In open daylight with other people around it seems a risk well worth taking.

The world (and our companies) would be a far better place if we chose to talk to more strangers, if only to say, 'Good morning'. It would also be a better place if we talked to people we do not like.

## BOX 31.1  Application of the HOW method of choice

**H**esitate    When a stranger crosses your path, hesitate. Ask yourself the question: 'Why shouldn't I greet this person and strike up a brief conversation?'

**O**utcome    Talking to strangers can have a useful purpose. Work out this purpose for yourself and keep reminding yourself of it

**W**ay    W-thinking: Set yourself a target. Extend the range of strangers you talk to. The following are some examples of situations in which complete strangers come 'within talking range':

- Visiting the restrooms
- Eating in the canteen
- Standing at the water cooler or coffee machine
- Riding in the elevator
- Just wandering around
- Travelling in aeroplanes, trains and buses

- Making purchases in a store
- Attending conferences and training programmes
- Standing in line and queueing to do something
- Waiting in the reception area when visiting a company
- Attending meetings with people from many departments
- When participating in games, quizzes and other activities
- Walking through an open-plan office area (or factory or warehouse etc.)

## THE CHOICE CHALLENGE

- Speak to at least three strangers today. (Over a period of time your life will change for the better as a result.)
- Speak to at least three people today who you know but whom you have not spoken to in the last three months. (The same applies.)

### Note

**1** Named after the good ship *The Mayflower* which in the year 1620c carried the first pilgrims from Southampton in the UK to 'settle' in America

CHAPTER THIRTY-TWO

# Choosing your 'self'

## Your 'self' is a product of all the choices you have made in life, no matter how small or large

## Being yourself

Who are you? To be successful you have to choose who you want to be. That is your choice. Unfortunately, if you do not make that conscious choice (and at work many people do not) someone will make it for you and you will become the same as everyone else: just another cog in the organization wheel that grinds away – and often grinds people down. You will be what someone else wants you to be.

I met a woman the other day who worked as a store assistant for a major retail chain. This is what she told me. 'I have worked for this company for 25 years and for 25 years my various managers have told me what to think, they have told me what to do and they have told me what to say (to customers). Now the new regime has come in and I am told to be myself, to think for myself. I am not used to that.'

You can easily identify people who work for this major retail chain. They all tend to dress the same way (when out of uniform), they all tend to groom themselves the same way, they all sound the same and they all tend to say the same types of thing. They are totally predictable because they all think the same way. They are total subscribers to the institution's way of doing things. But now things are changing. People are being told to be themselves and they are struggling with it. They are not used to it. It is so much easier to be what someone else wants you to be.

**It is so much easier to be what someone else wants you to be.**

The trouble is that many managers do not like people thinking for themselves; it creates trouble. As managers we want our employees to think like us and be like us in terms of what we want them to do. We do not want people to think differently or even behave differently because that just creates problems.

So people have to conform and follow convention. In doing so they become institutionalized and cease to be themselves. Employees become branded with the brand. They are the brand. When the brand is fresh and new that is great. The danger is that after 25 years the brand becomes jaded and tired. Customers become bored with the same old approach for the simple reason that frontline people have ceased to be themselves; they have become robots programmed to apply whatever the company wishes. It is mindless.

To please customers, to motivate others you must create your own mind and that means choosing your 'self'. You must choose what type of person you want to be. It means you must choose your own values, your own emotions, your own assumptions, your own attitudes, your own perceptions, your own rationales, your own criticisms, your own responses and your own behaviours. By doing so you become true to yourself. Listening to others and learning from others is vital to the process but is not the same as copying them and setting yourself up as an 'organization' man cloned by the system.

This idea is not new. Almost half a century ago William Whyte[1] wrote in his ground-breaking book: 'The organization man is one who has left home, spiritually as well as physically, to take the vows of organization life and it is they who are the mind and soul of our great self-perpetuating institutions.'

Choosing to be yourself means thinking for yourself and choosing what you want to be in life. It means choosing how you want to be seen by others. What it does not mean is being what others want you to be. That is too easy; you just follow the crowd, you blow with the wind, you run with the hares and hunt with the hounds. None of this requires too much spiritual effort; you just do what others do.

Choosing to be yourself requires energy on what can prove a tempestuous voyage of discovery. However, the outcome is wisdom, a quality which is highly underrated in this modern age.

Choosing to be yourself requires and produces wisdom. It requires reaching in the depths of your soul and discovering what you are really doing at work. What is the purpose of it all? Is it to purely to survive, is to make profit or is to accomplish something else? It is your choice. Choosing your self begs the questions of your behavioural choices and how these reflect the self you want to be.

The issue of choice is profound. The purpose of this book has been to challenge readers on those choices, to help people reflect on what they do in everyday life in terms of macro- and microbehaviours and on the extended range of possibilities available to them – but oft ignored.

These choices have deep significance to managers responsible for the conduct of a business or part of it. Too many managers get driven along by 'the organization system' without thinking too deeply about it and therefore without caring to develop it. Effective managers are those that are true to themselves rather than organization clones. These are the ones who gain respect and trust and motivate their teams to high performance. They are 'themselves' and this is reflected in all their macro- and microbehaviours.

| BOX 32.1 | Application of the HOW method of choice |
|----------|------------------------------------------|
| **H**esitate | Take a holiday (vacation) and enjoy an extended hesitation. Rediscover your 'self' by asking, Who am I? What is the real purpose of my work? What should I be as a manager? |
| **O**utcome | Ask yourself, 'When I retire or leave the company how do I want to be remembered? What is the outcome of all my efforts over the years?' (assuming you stay that long) |
| | Will I be happy with that outcome? More importantly will other people be happy too – with what I have made of myself? |
| **W**ay | W-thinking: The possibilities from which to choose your 'self' are endless. You can choose to continue as you are and be the |

same old self as you have always been. Or you can choose to develop yourself, to keep yourself fresh and new. There are millions of other options from which to choose in reflecting the self you want to be. The choice is yours

---

**THE CHOICE CHALLENGE**

- Choose to be yourself.
- Choose to develop yourself.
- Choose to go down in history as a good person who gave more than was taken.
- Choose to show this in everything you do, in all your macro- and microbehaviours.

**Note**

1 *Organization Man* by William H. Whyte, Simon & Schuster, 1956

# More power to your
# [ business-mind ]

Even at the end there's more we can learn. More that *we* can learn from your experience of this book, and more ways to add to *your* learning experience.

For who to read, what to know and where to go in the world of business, visit us at **business-minds.com**.

Here you can find out more about the people and ideas that can make you and your business more innovative and productive. Each month our e-newsletter, *Business-minds Express*, delivers an infusion of thought leadership, guru interviews, new business practice and reviews of key business resources directly to you. Subscribe for free at

● **www.business-minds.com/goto/newsletters**

Here you can also connect with ways of putting these ideas to work. Spreading knowledge is a great way to improve performance and enhance business relationships. If you found this book useful, then so might your colleagues or customers. If you would like to explore corporate purchases or custom editions personalised with your brand or message, then just get in touch at

● **www.business-minds.com/corporatesales**

We're also keen to learn from your experience of our business books – so tell us what you think of this book and what's on *your* business mind with an online reader report at business-minds.com. Together with our authors, we'd like to hear more from you and explore new ways to help make these ideas work at

● **www.business-minds.com/goto/feedback**

[ **www.business-minds.com**
www.financialminds.com ]